CONSUMER
protection

JON SUTHERLAND AND DIANE CANWELL

Hodder & Stoughton

A MEMBER OF THE HODDER HEADLINE GROUP

British Library Cataloguing in Publication Data
Sutherland, Jon
  Consumer protection
  1. Consumer protection – Great Britain   2. Consumer
  protection – Law and legislation – Great Britain
  I. Title   II. Canwell, Diane
  381.3'4'0941

ISBN 0 340 67407 5

First published 1996
Impression number   10 9 8 7 6 5 4 3 2 1
Year   1999 1998 1997 1996

Typeset by Fakenham Photosetting Limited, Fakenham,
Norfolk
Printed in Great Britain for Hodder & Stoughton Educational,
a division of Hodder Headline Plc, 338 Euston Road, London
NW1 3BH by The Bath Press

Contents

For Alistair

Acknowledgements

The authors would like to thank the following organisations for their help and support in the preparation and illustration of this book.

The Advertising Standards Authority
Allied Domecq plc
The British Electrotechnical Approvals Board
The British Standards Institute
The Central Statistical Office
The Consumers' Association
The Consumers in Europe Group
The Department of Trade and Industry
The Great Yarmouth and Waveney Health Authority
The Independent Television Commission
The Institute of Plumbing
The Mailing Preference Service
The Mid Suffolk District Council
The Office of Data Protection Registrar
The Office of Fair Trading
The Office of Water Services
Post Office Counters Ltd

Introduction

This optional unit Consumer Protection is linked very closely to the Mandatory Unit 3 Consumers and Customers. It focuses on the various forms of protection available to consumers as users and purchasers of services and products. In addition to understanding what protection is provided by legislation you will study organisations and charter initiatives established for the benefit of consumers. You will also study the consumerism movement and see how it provides a link between business and service organisations and consumers.

We have aimed through this book to cover the separate elements within the unit individually, and to cover the performance criteria and range in a logical and progressive way.

The student activities have been designed to provide evidence for portfolio building, as well as to give the student practical tasks to complete to help gain understanding of the topic being discussed.

We hope that you find the book a useful tool to the teaching and studying of Consumer Protection, and that the activities will be informative as well as interesting.

Jon Sutherland and Diane Canwell
1996

Examine Consumer Protection Law

Performance criteria

A student must:

1   explain the **objectives** of consumer law
2   describe **areas** of consumer protection legislation
3   explain **rights of consumers** from the key areas described
4   explain the **types of legal actions** which may result from non-compliance with consumer law

---

RANGE

Objectives: to protect, to ensure minimum standards, to inform, to regulate

Areas: control of credit, sale and supply of goods and services, safety, product liability, contractual terms

Rights of consumers: implied terms (sale of goods, provision of services), contents of credit agreements (cancellation, withdrawal from, termination of), restrictions (use of exclusion clauses, other contractual terms), compensation under product liability law

Types of legal actions: criminal, civil

Non-compliance: contractual, negligence

5.1.1 EXPLAIN THE OBJECTIVES OF CONSUMER LAW

OBJECTIVES

In this performance criteria we will investigate the variety of consumer law. This will include an introduction to the various areas of consumer protection as examples of consumer law.

We will be looking at the problem that exists, as any interaction between consumers and businesses could create a potential problem. The law, as we will see, serves both to protect the consumer and to support the *contract* which forms the basis of all agreements between consumers and businesses.

To protect

The consumer needs protection from certain businesses as there are numerous occasions when unscrupulous traders take advantage of their customers. As we will see, the relationship between consumers and businesses can become complicated, particularly if credit is involved. Equally, products and services sold should be of a sufficiently high quality so as to be durable enough, or relevant for, the purpose for which they were purchased.

Freedom to enter into contracts without any form of protection is best summed up by the Latin phrase *caveat emptor* (*let the buyer beware*). The situation has changed somewhat over the past few years and there are a number of laws that serve to protect and regulate these contracts.

Some people feel that contracts should be far clearer and more straightforward than simply implying certain rights and responsibilities. Criminal law handles this, as does administrative law. Indeed, criminal, civil and administrative law addresses certain aspects of the contract and how it is interpreted.

To ensure minimum standards

It is said that without a series of laws, even the minimum standards expected of a business would not be observed. Quality is the key to this, and with the drive towards quality standards and assurance, much of the risk has been taken out of the interaction between businesses and consumers. However, there are still many situations where minimum standards are not observed. It is in this respect that consumers need protection, and the legislation seeks to address this.

To inform

One of the other key roles or objectives of consumer law is to ensure that the public are aware of what they are buying and the applications of its use. Not only is there a legal obligation for the producers and the suppliers of products and services to have clear labelling, instructions and warnings, but the consumer protection law also seeks to clearly inform the public of their own rights and responsibilities in relation to the purchase and use of products and services.

To regulate

Regulators are independent people who are appointed by the government to control, mainly, the privatised monopoly companies such as British Gas. It is essential that these organisations exist to make sure that the companies do not misuse their powers, or unfairly control the supply of goods and services. They are also in place to ensure that these companies do not misuse their monopoly position, by attempting to keep other operators out of the market place.

**PC5.1.1
COM 2.1**

As a group, try to assess whose responsibility it would be to protect, ensure minimum standards, inform and regulate in respect of consumer law.

5.1.2 DESCRIBE AREAS OF CONSUMER PROTECTION LEGISLATION

AREAS OF CONSUMER PROTECTION LEGISLATION

In this performance criteria we look at the various areas related to consumer protection legislation. These include the following:

- the control of credit
- sale and supply of goods and services
- safety
- product liability
- contractual terms

We will consider each of these areas and identify the laws that relate to them.

Control of credit

The most common types of credit are:

- hire purchase
- credit
- charge cards
- finance company loans
- mail order catalogues
- pawn brokers
- money lenders

When you buy on credit, it usually means that you have to pay interest on top of the cash price. This is known as the APR (annual percentage rate of charge). The company offering the credit is required to quote the APR to show how expensive the credit actually is.

Let us have a look at some of the aspects of consumer credit and how the law regulates the actions of the supplier of credit and the consumer.

Hire purchase is a contract which allows the person having the goods (hirer) an option to purchase the goods at the end of the hire period. Throughout the hire period, the purchase price is paid in addition to the interest. The hirer pays this in instalments.

Credit sales are perhaps the most common form of credit that we use. The buyer takes possession of the goods straight away and is given time to pay for them. It is always a question of ownership; in this respect the ownership of the goods transfers to the new owner as soon as the goods are delivered.

Conditional sales are the main alternative to credit sales. Instead of the goods becoming the property of the buyer straight away, the goods do not transfer until a *condition* has been fulfilled. Obviously, the condition is that the buyer complete all of the instalments. The buyer has possession of the goods all of the time, from the beginning of the agreement. However, the buyer does not *own* the goods until all the payments have been made.

The Consumer Credit Act 1974 has brought all the various consumer credit agreements under one clear law. It lays down the following:

- it regulates the formation of credit agreements
- it regulates the terms of credit agreements
- it regulates the enforcement of credit agreements
- it insists that anyone offering credit should be licensed
- all advertisements concerning credit should show the cash price and the credit price so that the customer can see the difference
- there are conditions placed upon people offering credit door to door
- anyone offering credit without a licence can be prosecuted
- no one is exempt from the requirements of the Act

The Act also defines what is meant by a credit agreement. We will be looking at the contents of a credit agreement in performance criteria 5.1.3.

In 1964 a finance company repossessed a car without a court order. The debtor had paid more than a third of the price, so he was covered by protected goods rules. The company returned the car and the debtor used it for several months but refused to make any further payments. The finance company sued for payment and the debtor counter-claimed for the return of all of the money paid by him under the agreement.

As a group, try to assess which of the following happened:

> *it was held that the insurance company had wrongfully repossessed the car and could not correct the mistake so the debtor was entitled to repayment*

> *it was held that the debtor owed the outstanding payments from the agreement and that in the light of his not paying, the car was repossessed again*

Sale and supply of goods and services

Perhaps the most common type of transaction is the sale of goods. In all cases, whether you are buying goods and services from a shop, market stall or mail order company, you are entering into a contract with the seller.

The Sale of Goods Act (1979) applies to all of these contracts: it does not matter whether you are buying a chocolate bar or a car, the same rules apply.

What exactly is a contract for the sale of goods? If we refer to the Act itself, this is what it says:

> 'a contract by which the seller transfers or agrees to transfer the property in goods to the buyer for a money consideration called a price.'

This may sound very complicated and clumsy, but it is intended to make sure that all types of transactions are covered by the law. The main point of this statement is to make clear that exchanging goods or services for a price is different from swapping them or bartering for them. Remember, the word *goods* applies to all forms of goods, in-

CreditWise

Your guide to trouble-free credit...

Problems

Don't stop paying
Even if you've a major complaint about the goods don't stop your payments or you could end up in trouble. See the shop at once.

Debt collection
When you owe money, lenders are entitled to get you to pay. But they mustn't overdo it. If debt collectors start contacting your employer, knocking on your door every five minutes, or harassing you in any other way tell your consumer adviser.

Sky-high charges
If you think that you're paying sky-high interest charges see a consumer adviser. It might be worth your while to go to court and ask for the agreement to be changed to allow you to pay less. This is tricky, though, and you'll need expert advice.

Coping with debt

Never ignore demands for payment. It only means worse trouble.

Tell the lender as soon as you know you are in difficulties and try to work something out.

If you're in serious debt now, consult your consumer adviser or ask for the free booklet 'Debt - a survival guide'.

...They mustn't overdo it.

Fig. 5.1.1 CreditWise, *a useful booklet supplied by the Office of Fair Trading*

cluding services. It should be pointed out that money and land are not included under this Act.

Part-exchange deals are also covered under this Act, but the exchange of goods was not. This has now been addressed by the amended Sale and Supply of Goods Act (1994). Contracts that involve work and materials are also now covered under this Act which amended the Supply of Goods and Services Act (1982).

Focus study
The Prices Act 1974

This Act gives the Secretary of State for Trade and Industry the power to control the way in which prices are displayed on or near goods offered for sale.

Price marking orders may be made under the Act which require the seller to display the prices of the following:

- petrol
- fruit
- vegetables
- meat
- cheese
- food and drinks bought in restaurants

Typical examples of this Act mean that meat has to be displayed in terms of price per pound and petrol displayed in terms of price per gallon or per litre.

Safety

On 1 October 1987, as a part of the Consumer Protection Act, it became illegal (a criminal offence) to supply unsafe consumer goods in the UK. The suppliers of goods must make sure that they have taken all reasonable steps with regard to safety.

This law closes the gap in the existing safety legislation and states that an offence has been committed even if no one has been injured. If the supplier is found guilty of such a contravention of the law, then they can be fined up to £2,000 or six months in prison (sometimes both).

Unlike the laws covering product liability, the general safety requirements apply to all who supply the goods. Retailers have a special case here and providing they did not know, or had reasonable grounds for believing that the products were safe, they are not included under this law.

The Act covers all consumer goods. Although the following are not covered by the general safety requirements:

- crops
- water
- food
- aircraft and motor vehicles
- controlled drugs
- medicinal products
- tobacco

The definition of inadequate safety under the Act is a situation that increases the chance of death or injury.

All goods should be reasonably safe, having regard to the following circumstances:

- the way in which the goods are marketed
- the availability of instructions and warnings with the goods
- the published safety standards for those goods
- the costs of making the goods safer

Any supplier who does not meet the general safety requirements will not be committing an offence under the following circumstances:

- the goods conform with EC obligations
- the goods conform to safety regulations or safety standards that have been approved by the government in terms of general safety
- the goods were intended for export
- the goods were not supplied new (and not for hire)
- the goods were supplied by a retailer who did not have grounds to suspect they were unsafe
- all reasonable steps had been taken to ensure the supplier was not committing an offence

Some safety standards are set by the government to act as a *benchmark* for general safety requirements. There is a comprehensive range of standards that aim to make sure goods comply with an approved standard. This list of approved standards is available through the Department of Trade and Industry.

Fig. 5.1.2 The BSI kite mark ensures that the product complies in every way with the appropriate British Standard

Fig. 5.1.3 The kite mark of the British Electrotechnical Approvals Board for Household Products

▼

Focus study
British Standards

British Standards aim to set out the requirements necessary to ensure that a material, product or procedure is fit for its intended purpose.

These standards lay down an agreed level of quality to ensure that products are fit for the purpose for which they are designed and explain how they are tested.

Laboratories test each product in the same way so that the results can be compared on a uniform basis. Within this, the technical language and symbols used can be understood by all those concerned.

The Codes of Practice lay down the best accepted practice for operators, such as the installation and maintenance of equipment and provision of services.

The target for the production of a British Standard is 12 months, but in cases where the subject is very complicated it may take longer.

▼

Focus study
Kite marks

Kite marks are the certification trademarks of the British Standards Institution (BSI). You will find the kite mark on many industrial and some consumer goods. The kite mark shows that the product complies in every way with the appropriate British Standard. The kite mark supports the manufacturer's claim that the product meets the British Standard.

Remember that the kite mark is only a safety mark and not a guarantee of quality.

▼

Focus study
BSI Testing Centre

Based in Hemel Hempstead, the Testing Centre carries out regular tests on manufactured goods for the kite mark and other approval schemes. It also sends inspectors to check on the factories where the goods are produced.

Typical examples of the articles tested include:

- car seat belts
- children's safety seats
- cycle rear lamps
- mattresses
- oil heaters
- protective helmets
- thermometers
- office machinery (for electrical safety)
- toys and fabrics (especially for flammability)
- TV receivers

The Consumer Protection Act aims to improve the regulations found under the previous consumer safety laws. It makes it possible for the government to make regulations quickly when it thinks the public needs to be protected.

The government (via the Secretary of State) can issue 'prohibition notices' which prevent named suppliers from supplying particular goods that have been shown to be unsafe. The Secretary of State can also issue warnings, requiring named suppliers to include warnings (at their own expense) about unsafe goods that they have supplied.

Enforcement of the safety legislation is mainly the responsibility of the trading standards offices. They make test purchases and are entitled to search premises to obtain information and evidence. They can issue suspension notices, prohibiting suppliers from selling goods that they believe break the safety legislation, and can apply to the magistrates' court in order to seize goods and destroy them.

The producers and the importers can, of course, appeal against the suspension and seizure of goods. They can also apply for compensation for the costs imposed upon them in particular circumstances. Customs Offices may also hold goods at the port of entry (for up to two days) to allow the enforcement agencies time to make enquiries regarding the safety of the goods.

The Data Protection Act 1984 has had enormous implications for all organisations who have access to or store information about their customers and employees. An individual about whom an organisation has information stored does have specific rights. These include:

- access to that information
- the right to challenge inaccurate information

If an organisation fails to comply with the Data Protection Act in this respect, then the individual affected has a right to be compensated.

There are some exceptions to this. These are:

- where the individual has supplied the information themselves
- where the organisation has taken *all reasonable care* to acquire the information
- where the information relates to payroll matters
- where the information relates to pension details
- where the information is used only for statistical purposes and, in addition it does not specifically identify individuals

The Data Protection Act attempts to ensure that stored information is only put to specific lawful purposes. While it is difficult to maintain this degree of certainty about the use of the information, most organisations tend to use stored information for its specifically stated purpose only. Problems will inevitably arise when there is an interchange of this information between different organisations. The organisation which initially collected the data may have had a specific purpose in mind. However, the organisation which has acquired the information may have different motives altogether. The transmission of sensitive information from one organisation to another can pose considerable problems both to the individual and to the Data Protection Registrar. In particular, information stored regarding an individual's creditworthiness may include a number of inaccuracies which have not been identified. If the individual subsequently discovers that inaccuracies have been made, then it is a difficult task to trace

the transmission and use of the original inaccurate information in order to correct it.

**PC5.1.2
COM 2.1**

student activity

00:15

▌*nformation regarding customers is regularly traded between organisations. How would an organisation ensure that the information being passed on does not adversely affect the individual or the organisation itself? Discuss this in pairs.*

As with any data storage facility, the organisation will take steps to ensure that unauthorised access is avoided. The Data Protection Act, however, makes this a legal requirement and therefore, unauthorised access can mean fines for the organisation which has suffered the breach of security. The sensitivity of some of the material stored is such that it could be used for criminal or other unlawful purposes by an unauthorised entrant. The sensitivity of the information is further heightened by the fact that the individual whose information is stored in the system may be unaware that it is actually there. If unauthorised entry is gained and this information is used by others, then the individual may suffer as a result.

Most organisations keep detailed records which may include the following:

- customers' names and addresses
- customer transactions
- customer credit information
- specific information regarding customers, such as their political affiliations (in recent years certain high street banks have admitted that they keep details of customers' political allegiances)
- staff records
- personal information regarding employees' domestic situations
- disciplinary action taken against employees

Organisations obviously store a great deal more information than this, but the Data Protection Act relates specifically to the way in which this information is used. The Act attempts to prevent this information being used to harm an individual. The Act requires all organisations or individuals who

hold on computer personal details regarding other individuals, to register with the Data Protection Registrar. If an organisation or individual fails to do this, then they may be fined up to £2,000. The Registrar needs to know the following:

- what sort of information is held
- what use is made of the information
- who else has access to this information
- what methods were used to collect the information

The Registrar must ensure that the data conforms to the Act. Specifically, this means that the Registrar must ensure that the information complies with the following codes:

- the information has been collected in an open and fair manner
- the information is only held for lawful purposes
- the uses to which the information is put are disclosed to the Registrar
- the information held is relevant to the purpose for which it is held
- the information is accurate
- the information is up to date
- any irrelevant or inaccurate information is destroyed
- individuals can be told about the existence of the information
- individuals can challenge inaccurate information
- the information is kept confidential
- the organisation takes steps to ensure that unauthorised access is avoided

**PC5.1.2
COM 2.1, 2.2**

student activity

00:30

Consider the Data Protection Act from a personal point of view, and try to assess the range and amount of information about yourself which may be stored by organisations. Write a list of any considerations you can think of and then compare your list to those of the remainder of your group. How much do they vary?

The fifth principle of the Data Protection Act states that:

'personal data shall be accurate and, where necessary, kept up to date'

The Act gives further guidance on interpreting this principle. *Accurate* means correct and not misleading as to any matter of fact. An opinion, which does not purport to be a statement of fact, cannot be challenged on the grounds of inaccuracy.

The Act contains special provisions which apply to information obtained from the data subject or from third parties. These are dealt with fully within the Act. Stated briefly, a data user who wishes to rely on these provisions must ensure that both the fact that the information has come from such a source and any challenge by the data subject to the accuracy of the information are recorded.

If these requirements are complied with, the fact that the personal data are inaccurate does not result in a breach of this principle.

The Registrar will seek to establish that there is a factual inaccuracy and will also wish to see whether the data user has taken all responsible steps to prevent the inaccuracy. The matters which they may wish to consider will include:

- the significance of the inaccuracy
- the source from which the inaccurate information was obtained
- any steps taken to verify the information
- the procedures for data entry and for ensuring that the system itself does not introduce inaccuracies into the data
- the procedures followed by the data user when the inaccuracy came to light

If an individual suffers damage because of inaccurate personal data held about them by a user, they are entitled to claim compensation from the data user. An application for compensation must be made by the individual to the court. The Registrar cannot award compensation.

In order to decide whether or not the Data Protection Act affects the activities of an organisation, it will have to be considered whether the organisation uses any of the following:

- word processors
- microcomputers
- minicomputers
- mainframe computers

In making this decision, the organisation should remember that it makes no difference whether the equipment is owned or leased. It is not the equipment itself that is important, but the use of that equipment for the storage and processing of data. The control of the data is in the hands of the organisation.

If any of the above are used by the organisation, then the following questions need to be addressed:

- is the equipment used for the processing of accounts payable and accounts received?
- is the equipment used for the checking of credit ratings?
- is the equipment used for the payroll and storage of personnel data?
- is the equipment used for marketing and sales information?
- is the equipment used for the storage of general management information?
- is the equipment used for the production and manipulation of letters and text?
- is the equipment used for the transmission of electronic mail?

If the organisation does use their equipment for any of the above, then these activities need not be considered for restriction by the legislation.

On the other hand, if the organisation can identify that it stores and uses personal data and has to ensure that it is properly secured, then this does require special attention:

the data protection laws frequently refer to specific types of personal data which are either prohibited or must have special safeguards, as detailed earlier. This data relates to:

- racial origin
- political opinions
- religious beliefs
- health

It does not affect the responsibility of the organisation to ensure that personal data is only processed in a properly controlled environment if they use a computer service bureau. The computer service bureau has to register that it provides processing services to other organisations, and must conform to the requirements laid down for security and confidentiality.

If an organisation's computer system holds any data regarding the following, then it must ensure that it is conforming to specific domestic legislation:

- the sexual life of employees
- any criminal convictions of employees
- the colour of skin of employees
- the use of intoxicants by employees
- the intimacy of the private life of its employees
- the trade union membership or otherwise of its employees

The personal data held by the data user may include information which identifies another individual as well as the data subject: for example, a relative or associate of the data subject or a person who has given information to the data user about the data subject. In replying to a data subject request, the data user need not disclose the information unless the other individual has consented to the disclosure. The data user, however, must still give as much information as possible to the data subject without revealing the other individual's identity. This may involve editing the information to remove names or other identifying details. Information should not be withheld under this provision merely because the data user suspects that the data subject may be able to guess the other individual's identity. The provision applies only where anyone lacking the data subject's special knowledge could reasonably be expected to identify the other individual from the information.

The fact that another individual's consent may be required should never prevent the data user from replying at least partially to the request. When he/she has received the request, together with enough information about identity and location, the data user should therefore always reply within 40 days. The reply should consist of:

- confirmation that personal data about that individual are held
- a copy of as much of the information as can be given without disclosing the identity of the other individual who has not consented

Obviously, one of the negative effects of the implementation of the Data Protection Act for an organisation could be the costs involved.

If the organisation is large and the amount of information stored is of a nature to require registration with the Registrar, then some expense will be involved in the overseeing of the input of such data. It may be necessary for the organisation to employ an individual to control and monitor this process. Such a Data Protection Officer would have the responsibility of monitoring the additions, deletions and use of information. This could involve the organisation in a great deal of time in man hours and expense in terms of salary.

PC5.1.2
COM 2.1, 2.4

Again, as in the previous activity, obtain copies of the guidelines regarding the implementation of the Data Protection Act. You will find that your college or local library will have copies. Try to estimate the cost to an organisation of complying with the legislation. Does it cost more for an organisation than it does for an individual? Discuss your findings with the remainder of your group.

Health and Safety at Work Act 1974 and EC Directives on Health and Safety

Before this Act, employees were protected against hazardous working conditions under a number of different pieces of legislation. HASAW aimed to bring all these together and extend the protection of employees under a single Act. The main points of the Act are:

- it stated general duties of an employer across all types of industry and commerce

PC5.1.2
COM 2.2, 2.4
IT 2.1, 2.2, 2.3

There are several exemptions and restrictions set down in the guidelines relating to the Data Protection Act. Obtain a copy of these leaflets and research the following:

- *what data is exempt from the regulations?*
- *what disclosures are prohibited by law?*
- *how likely is it that data relating to one individual could be accessed and purchased by another individual or organisation?*

Present your findings in the form of a word processed report.

An introduction to The Data Protection Act

Fig. 5.1.4 Cover to the leaflet What is Data Protection?
*supplied by the Office of the Data Protection
Registrar*

- it created a system by which HASAW could be enforced (by the Health and Safety Executive and local authorities)
- it created the Health and Safety Commission which aimed to help employers understand the regulations and develop codes of practice
- it was backed up by the imposition of a series of legal obligations on the employer, who risked facing criminal proceedings for failure to follow them
- it imposed minimum safety regulations, and introduced improvements to the working environment

The work of HASAW has been followed up by a number of EC directives covering such areas as safety signs at work, employees handling hazardous materials and guidance regarding avoidance of major hazards.

New regulations and codes of practice are being designed continually and now cover nearly all work activities, both in the private and the public sector. Steps are now being taken to cover any gaps in the legislation, or to make it easier to understand and implement.

Management of Health and Safety at Work Regulations 1992

This major piece of legislation aims to provide a systematic and well-organised set of guidelines in relation to health and safety. They include the following:

11

- employers are required to assess any potential risks employees may have to face and take preventive measures to cope with them
- this risk assessment must be continually monitored by a group of employers working closely with at least five employees
- employers are required to employ specialists whose sole responsibility it is to implement the preventive measures, as well as to provide information for all other employees within the organisation
- employers are further required to carry out regular screenings of their employees to make sure that they have not suffered any ill-effects as a result of carrying out their duties. If appropriate, any health hazards which have been identified should be addressed immediately.
- employees who have been given the duties of Safety Representatives should be regularly consulted, provided with time and space to carry out their investigations, and given the authority to act on them

Health and Safety (Display Screen Equipment) Regulations 1992

This legislation is designed to protect employees who spend considerable amounts of their working hours in front of a computer screen. The main points of the legislation are:

- employees must receive sufficient breaks from the screen
- work should not be repetitive and the employee should be given a variety of tasks
- basic safety requirements must be satisfied as regards the screen itself and the design of the keyboard, as well as the shape and height of the desk and chair being used
- regular eye tests must be provided by the employer, and if the employee needs special spectacles in order to carry out his/her tasks, these should be provided by the employer
- efficient lighting should be provided in the room where the employee is using the computer, as should proper ventilation

The Factories Act 1961

This Act covers a wide range of different organisations, focusing on the use of machinery. The key features of this piece of legislation are:

- the employer must provide toilet and washing facilities
- premises should be adequately heated and ventilated
- the employer must make sure that floors, stairs and passageways are not obstructed in any way
- all floors should have a non-slippery surface
- potentially dangerous machinery should be fenced off to protect employees
- the employer must ensure there are adequate fire escapes, well sign-posted and regularly maintained
- fire doors themselves should never be locked or obstructed

The Offices, Shops and Railway Premises Act 1963

This Act concentrates on conditions within shops and offices and provides a number of clear guidelines to the employer, including:

- in work areas, the temperature must never drop below 16 °C
- the employer must ensure that there is an adequate supply of fresh air
- following on from the Factories Act 1961, this legislation states that the employer must provide enough toilet and washing facilities in relation to the number of staff. He/she must also make sure that there is hot and cold running water as well as soap and clean towels
- again, following on from the Factories Act 1961, this legislation states that an employer has to provide suitable lighting wherever employees are expected to work or move around
- the employer must ensure that there is at least 12 square metres of working space per employee

Product liability

There are countless cases of people being injured by defective products, and they may have the right to sue for damages. The term *product liability* is given to the laws that govern these rights.

In the past, the injured person had to prove the manufacturer was negligent, but the Consumer Protection Act of 1987 gives the injured person the right to sue a supplier without having to prove negligence under the sale-of-goods law. It is also worth remembering that this also applied to individuals who have been injured, regardless of the fact that they did not have the product sold to them.

When a person is injured, action can be taken against one (or more) of the following:

- the producers or manufacturers of the product
- the importers of the product (strictly speaking the importers of the product into the EC)
- the suppliers of own-brand products
- wholesalers and retailers who do not disclose the true producer of the product

Liability under the Consumer Protection Act is not just restricted to consumer products. With the exception of unprocessed agricultural products and buildings, all other products are covered (including those used at work). With regard to buildings, the materials used are covered (e.g this would include the bricks, cement and wood).

A defective product is strictly defined as one where the safety of that product is not as the person who is using it should expect. A product is not defective just because it is of poor quality, nor is it defective if there is a safer version on the market.

When looking at a defective product, the court will consider the following:

- the way in which the product is marketed
- any instructions that might be given (or warnings)
- what the product should be reasonably used for
- the time that the producer supplied the product

Warnings and instructions should be made clear, particularly in cases when it is known that the product is misused. A good example of this would be solvents.

An injured person can sue under the Act for compensation. The guidelines are:

- if the product has resulted in a death
- if the product has resulted in injury
- if the damage has resulted in the loss of property that is valued at more than £275

It still remains the responsibility of the injured person (or plaintiff) to show that the defect in the product has caused the damage.

The producer or importer can attempt to avoid the liability of the alleged defective product by proving one of the following:

- that he/she did not actually supply the product in question (perhaps it was stolen or is a copy of their product)

- that the scientific and technical knowledge at the time the product was supplied did not suggest that the product was defective
- that the defect was a result of having to comply with the law. The producer/supplier will need to show that the law actually meant the product was inevitably defective
- that the defect came about after the product had been supplied (for example the retailer may not have taken reasonable steps to avoid damage or defects)
- that the supplier is not actually a business. This includes products that are made at home (not for resale or second-hand goods)
- that the defect occurred as a result of a component made by another producer being defective

In all cases, the plaintiff must begin the court action within three years of being injured by the defective product. The injured person cannot sue under the Act three years after the defective product was supplied by the producer (e.g this refers to old stock in a retail outlet)

GUIDE TO
THE CONSUMER PROTECTION ACT 1987

Product Liability and Safety Provisions

Consumer Safety Unit

dti

the department for Enterprise

Fig. 5.1.5 Guide to the Consumer Protection Act 1987, focusing on product liability and safety provisions provided by the Consumer Safety Unit of the DTI

Contractual terms

Contracts contain the express and implied conditions and warranties which are known as the terms of the contract. Basically, these set out the rights and obligations of both parties entering the contract.

There are often conditions attached to the contract and if either side breaks these conditions, then it is reasoned that the contract is at an end. In simple terms, if the goods are returned to the seller, then the buyer is entitled to get their money back.

Warranties are another aspect of the contract, less important than the conditions, but the buyer still has the right to sue if there is a difference in the value between what the buyer paid for and what he/she actually got. The seller of the goods and services may impose certain limitations or conditions in order to exclude liability for a breach of the conditions and warranties. The buyer may often not be in a position to refuse these, so the buyer is protected under common law and other legislations. This, as we will see later, means that the seller cannot include clauses in the contract that could be considered to be unfair.

It is, perhaps, the appropriate point to have a look, in detail, at the nature of a contract and see how important it is in real terms.

Basically, a contract is an agreement. Any contract consists of five main elements. These are the:

- offer
- acceptance
- consideration
- intention
- capacity

These are common to all the types of contract regardless of the nature of the contract itself.

Offer

The person, or organisation, making the offer is called the offeror. The party to whom the offer is made is known as the offeree. The offer is a statement about the proposed terms of the offer. Once the offer is accepted, then the agreement is binding. If either side now fails to do as they have promised, then this is a breach of the contract. This is common law, a series of understandings that have been developed over many years. At one point in the past, a judge has made a decision about the nature of the contract and the legal standing involved.

It should be remembered that price tags or displays in windows are not offers, they are called *invitations to treat*. Similarly, a classified advertisement *offering* something for sale is not, strictly speaking, an offer. It, too, is an invitation to treat. On the other hand, if you offered £25 to someone who could find your lost cat, and they did, you are promising to pay them for their effort.

Acceptance

Acceptance is the second stage of the contract. This obviously means that the offeree is accepting the terms of the contract. A conditional offer, such as those that you see on houses for sale *subject to contract*, means there are conditions and offers. The offeree needs to find out and confirm various things by using a surveyor or a solicitor, before eventually accepting the conditions of the contract from the offeror.

Once the offeree decides to accept the contract, they need to communicate this to the offeror as they will need to know that they are now party to the agreement.

Consideration

Consideration is the technical term used to describe the *contribution* each party makes to the deal. In other words, if you promise to pay £12.99 for a particular CD, then the shop promises to supply the named CD. If one side does not get what was promised by the other party, then this is a breach of the contract. However, if you promise something for which you receive nothing in return, then you can break your promise as this is not a contract. It is important to realise that the promises have been developed over the years in the interests of fairness. There are further complications which arise out of extra payments and part-payments, but those tend to involve employment, so they are not considered here.

Intention

The fourth part of a simple contract is the intention to be legally bound. In order to help the courts decide whether either party intended to be legally bound by the contract, the following aspects have been developed over the years:

within social or domestic situations there is no intention to be legally bound. If, for example, you are promised by a parent to be paid £5 per week if you do all of the washing up, they are not legally bound to pay you

in commercial situations, there is always an intention to be legally bound. Regardless of the fact that some payments may be goodwill ones or *ex-gratia* payments, this is not sufficient reason to assume that either side was not intending to be legally bound

Capacity

The law also protects those who are not in full control of their faculties. The mentally ill, for example, can avoid liability in contractual terms if the other party can be seen to be aware of the fact that they were incapable at the time of signing. Even the insane, who may not show outward signs of their incapacity, are not excused from their

contractual obligations if the other party was unaware of their mental disorder. Similarly, those under the age of 18 are also closely protected. Contracts involving minors fall under the following headings:

- **valid binding contracts** – which are made for necessities or beneficial contracts of service. The lesson here is not to sell children what they do not need
- **beneficial contract of service** – these include such things as apprenticeship agreements. When the agreement is regarded as a whole, it must be reasonable and for the minor's benefit
- **valid but voidable contracts** – this category includes contracts concerning land, buying shares, partnership agreements and marriage settlements. In other words if the individual is a minor, then none of these contracts are applicable, although they are, in themselves, valid contracts

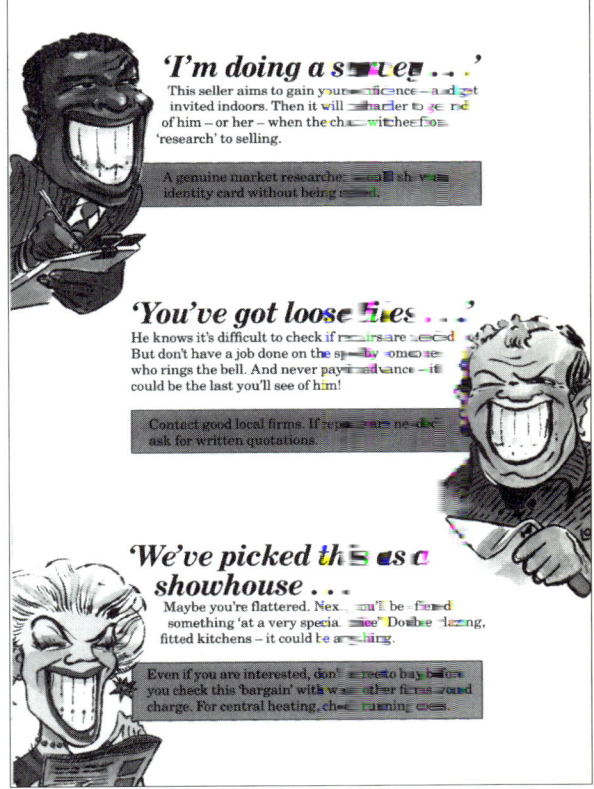

Fig. 5.1.6 The Office of Fair Trading's How to Cope with Doorstep Salesmen *also contains useful information on coping with phone callers*

Focus study
Phone sales

Reputable companies will always identify themselves and say clearly why they are selling. In some cases, the caller may be trying to sell directly to you, or they may be attempting to arrange an appointment.

It is always wise to take time and think it over, even if you are interested. A reputable organisation will always offer to call you back, or if you prefer, give you their number so that you can contact them.

Whenever the question of credit or hire purchase arises, beware, as there is no cooling off period to cancel it once you have signed a form.

These guidelines are supported by the Direct Selling Association, the British Direct Marketing Association and the Glass and Glazing Federation.

PC5.1.2
COM 2.1

As a group, try to come up with at least 10 examples of different types of organisation which would either phone or call personally to your home in an attempt to sell you products and services.

5.1.3 EXPLAIN RIGHTS OF CONSUMERS FROM THE KEY AREAS DESCRIBED

RIGHTS OF CONSUMERS

This performance criteria aims to help you develop an understanding of the individual's rights as a consumer and the need for credit agreements. This can be a complicated area, and at all times we have restricted the depth of information to the absolute minimum.

Implied terms (sale of goods, provision of services)

As the concept and reality of consumerism has grown in importance, there has, quite naturally, been a demand for consumer rights. There have been numerous changes over the years to increase the protection.

One of the biggest problems is creating a broad enough law to cover all of the various transactions and sales of both goods and services. There needed to be rules upon which all trade could be conducted. In the early years, these laws did not really cater for the buyer. All the laws stated was that the seller promised the buyer that the goods were of a particular quality. This was known as *merchantable quality*. The seller, quite naturally, never made any claims about the goods that might cause them problems later if they did not match up to the stated claims. The overriding philosophy was again *caveat emptor*: 'Let the buyer beware!'

The consumer or the buyer was not getting a good deal based on this approach. Not only were the wishes and needs of the buyer being ignored by the seller, but the seller normally put into the contract several *exclusion clauses*, or ways of avoiding being held liable for selling goods that were not of merchantable quality. At the time, the sellers were not breaking the law. However, the buyers were being sold goods that they could not give back to the seller if they were defective. By 1973, this had all changed and the seller was no longer able to put exclusion clauses into the contract to avoid their liability. The goods had to be of merchantable quality.

The problem appeared to be solved, but the sellers, aware that consumers did not really understand the nature of the contracts, continued to put in exclusion clauses. Whenever this was tested, the courts simply ignored the exclusion clauses. Nevertheless, something else had to be done.

In 1978, the law changed again. The Consumer Transactions (Restrictions on Statement) Order made it illegal to put in exclusion clauses. If a seller did, then this was a criminal offence. For the most part, this did the trick.

In 1979, the Sale of Goods Act set out the statutory implied terms (sections 12–15). Implied terms are basically promises made by the seller to the buyer. The important thing to realise is that if the seller makes these promises, then the buyer has the right to cancel the contract, reject the goods and claim (sue) for damages. This is particularly the case in respect of warranties.

These restrictions from the Act are a part of all contracts for the sale of goods. There are two other Acts to remember, and this now means that all contracts are covered in the same way. These are:

- the Supply of Goods (Implied Terms) Act 1973
- the Supply of Goods and Services Act 1982

Let us have a look at those sections from the 1979 Act in a little more detail:

Section 12

One of the key implied conditions of a sale is that the seller has the right to sell the goods. If, for example, the goods sold to a buyer had been stolen, then the buyer has the right to cancel the contract and get a full refund from the seller. This also holds true for copyrights and other forms of ownership known as *intellectual property rights*.

You cannot sell something under the name or label owned by a third party. A car company could not sell copies of Ford cars, simply changing the name of their car to Ford. The main point of all of this is to ensure that the seller does not sell any goods that a third party may have some kind of claim over. The buyer is, therefore, assured that they have complete ownership of the goods.

Section 13

This section refers to the description of the goods. It is true to say that we all buy the majority of our purchases based on the description alone. If we buy a can of baked beans, we expect baked beans to be in there and not something else. This description also includes:

- weight
- size
- ingredients/components
- age

If a car dealer sold a car that had its true mileage changed, then it would be both in breach of section 13 and breaking the Trade Descriptions Act (1968). If there are only minor differences between the description and the actual nature of the goods, then this is often ignored.

However, if there are differences between the description and the real nature of the goods, the buyer can reject the goods, even if they did not suffer as a result.

Section 14

The actual Act clearly states the following in respect of faulty goods or those which are not of merchantable quality:

'where the seller sells goods in the course of a business there is an implied condition that the goods supplied under the contract are of merchantable quality.'

▼

Focus study
The Unsolicited
Goods and Services
Act 1971

Traders can be fined if they demand payment for goods they have supplied that the consumer did not order.

If a consumer receives unsolicited goods which are not collected by the sender within six months, then they become the property of the consumer.

If the consumer writes to the seller asking for the goods to be collected and the goods are still not collected, then after 30 days they become the property of the consumer.

It goes on to say:

'except that there is no such condition:

(a) as regards defects specifically drawn to the buyers' attention before the contract is made; or

(b) if the buyer examines the goods before the contract is made, as regards defects'

The key features of this part of the 1979 Act are:

- the seller must be a business as these implied conditions do not apply to private sales
- it does not matter which part of the distribution chain the seller is at
- the conditions do not apply if the defect has been pointed out to the buyer before the sale, or, indeed, when the buyer has looked at the goods before purchasing them and should have discovered that they were defective
- in complying with this section the seller needs to have a quality control system. This is particularly the case if the seller is the manufacturer

In terms of merchantable quality, as we have mentioned earlier, section 14(6) states:

'goods of any kind are of merchantable quality if they are as fit for the purpose or purposes for which the goods of that kind are commonly bought as it is reasonable to expect having regard to any description applied to them, the price (if relevant) and all other relevant circumstances.'

This is a rather convoluted way of saying that although the quality of the goods may vary, they should be reasonably fit for the ordinary uses to which they are put. If the seller describes them as *rejects* or *seconds* then the buyer must understand what this means. It should also be remembered that you can buy a pair of shoes for £10 or £100. You should not, necessarily, expect the cheaper shoes to be of the same quality as the more expensive ones.

Also under this section of the Act the packaging needs to be of a sufficient quality in order to en-sure that the product is safely contained and will not leak or burst. There have even been cases when an ingredient or a chemical used in a product has caused the buyer to suffer or suffer damages. In these cases the seller could be liable.

In 1987 the Law Commission published a report which recommended that the sellers' obligations in relation to merchantable quality be clarified. To this end, the term *merchantable quality* was replaced by the phrase *acceptable quality*. This rather broader and vaguer statement allows for the different levels of price and other circumstances which may affect the quality of the product.

With regard to *fitness for a notified purpose*, the seller may find themselves liable if the goods are not fit for a special or unusual purpose. Bearing in mind that many buyers rely on the seller to give them expert information about a product, it should be expected that the product will, in fact, perform as the seller describes. Having said this, the seller cannot be held liable if the buyer puts the product to a peculiar use, or suffers from a rare disorder or allergy which is aggravated by the product.

student activity 00:15

PC5.1.3
COM 2.1

A *buyer purchased a quantity of canned food from a wholesaler. The contract stated that each case would contain 30 cans. On delivery the buyer discovered that about half of the cases were packed with only 24 cans. What should be the outcome of this problem? Discuss as a group.*

Contents of credit agreements (cancellation, withdrawal from, termination of)

There are various types of credit, not just the credit agreement: overdrafts or loans are just as common. However, we will be concentrating on credit agreements.

If you chose to buy something on credit, you

have extra rights. If you pay over £100 for something by credit, then the lender becomes equally liable if anything goes wrong with it and you can make a claim against them.

There are special rules which apply when you purchase something on credit at home. A contract is made, just like under other circumstances, but the customer has five days to change their minds if they wish.

It is always a good idea to check the cancellation rights before the credit deal is signed. This will allow the person taking the credit to cancel it if they change their minds. The problem is that the time limits are often quite tight so the person taking the credit will need to move fast.

There are some rules about cancelling the credit, which are:

- you signed the agreement at home rather than on the premises of the supplier or the lender
- you signed the credit deal in the last few days
- you agreed the terms of the credit not by phone but in person with the lender

---

▼

Focus study
Credit cards

Credit card law reforms proposed by the Office of Fair Trading offer no significant new benefits for card holders and weaken some of their existing rights, say consumer groups.

Under the Consumer Credit Act as it now stands, people who pay by credit card for goods or services worth at least £100 which turn out to be faulty, or which are never received because the supplier goes bust, are entitled to claim a full refund from the credit card issuer. The credit card issuer is held equally liable with the supplier for your loss. You can claim the full cost of the item, even if you have only paid a *deposit* by card and the balance in cash or by cheque.

Card issuers had lobbied hard to reduce the protection in this area by switching to *second-in-line liability* under which consumers would only be able to claim compensation from the card company once they had pursued their claim against the supplier.

In his second report on *consumer lender liability* (detailed in section 75 of the Act), the Director-General of the Office of Fair Trading has turned down this request and confirms that credit card issuers should remain *jointly and severally liable* with suppliers for losses suffered by their customers. He has also restated his view that card companies are legally required to honour claims for goods purchased abroad. In the past the major card issuers have always argued that their liability does not extend to claims arising out of the £3 billion spent on overseas card transactions annually.

However, card issuing members of the Credit Card Research Group and the Association of Payment Clearing Services have agreed to take part in a voluntary scheme. This scheme compels them to meet claims up to the amount of credit granted on an *ex gratia* basis, from now until the end of 1996, when the matter will be reviewed. But in order to pull the major card issuers into line, the Director-General (DG) has had to make some compromises which, according to the National Consumer Council (NCC), weaken consumer rights.

The DG is proposing that claims against card issuers should be limited to the amount of credit involved in the transaction – something the card companies have wanted, to reduce their exposure to unpredictable losses.

The NCC condemns this as a backward step for consumers, as they would no longer be able to reclaim from their credit card company the entire cost of a faulty product or service and compensation for personal injury or damage to property. Instead, they would only be able to claim the amount of credit given, with no compensation.

The DG has also ignored strong representations from the NCC to scrap the lower £100 cash limit for claims. However, the NCC says:

'Consumers who buy unsafe goods and suffer
injury or damage could make good use of the
protection of Section 75 and should not be
inhibited by an arbitrary lower limit on either
cash value or credit extended. Many of the most
dangerous goods are the cheapest ones.'

Appliances like kettles and irons would not be covered, for example. The Consumers' Association is less critical of the proposals, having feared a far worse reduction in consumer rights.

Focus study
The Consumer Credit Public Register

The Consumer Credit Public Register holds applications for holders of consumer credit licences. These licences, granted by the Office of Fair Trading, are open to the public.

The information on the registers covers:

- licences which have been given up by traders
- licences which have been revoked or suspended by the Office of Fair Trading (OFT)
- decisions made by the OFT about particular licences or applications and the outcome of the appeals

Consumer Credit Act 1974

Fig. 5.1.7 Detailing the duties of the Consumer Credit Public Register under the Consumer Credit Act 1974, this leaflet explains how to make an enquiry

- exemptions from parts of the Consumer Credit Act
- orders in respect of agreements by traders who made credit agreements without being licensed

Licence holders and applicants are listed on a computer index, and the public can either visit, phone, or write in, for information.

Focus study
Credit reference agencies

Whenever a customer seeks credit, the credit shop or loan company will need to check that they are not a bad risk. For convenience, they use information-collecting organisations called *credit reference agencies* (CRAs).

In some cases, the loan companies use a system called *credit scrutiny*. The customer scores points for the information given on the application form. The customer can be turned down if they do not get enough points.

Individuals have the legal right to know the name and address of the CRA that was asked about their background. This must be done within 28 days of your last contact with them, and they must give you the name and address within seven days.

The information stored by the main agencies (on every adult in the UK) includes the following:

- *the electoral or voters roll:* if your address is on the roll, this proves that you live at the address given on the application form
- *a record of county court judgements and bankruptcies*: which include details of all people taken to court for not paying their debts. Even if the debt has been paid, then the agencies keep a judgement on file for six years
- *a record of previous credit given*: which shows how well (or badly) debts have been paid in the past

You can write to the CRAs and request to see your file. Although the CRAs may need additional information, they must reply within seven days.

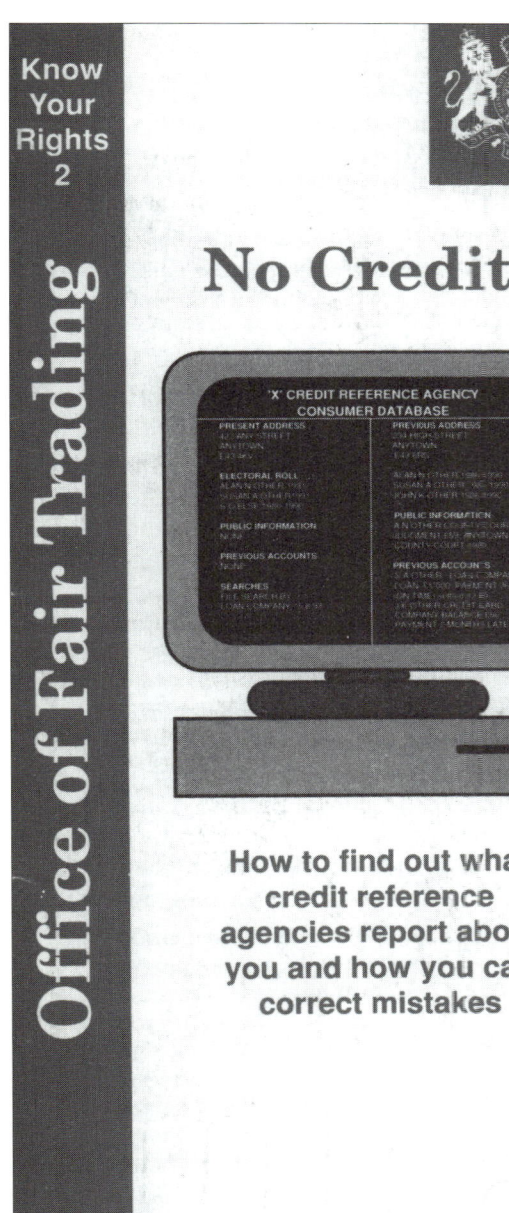

Know Your Rights 2

Office of Fair Trading

No Credit?

How to find out what credit reference agencies report about you and how you can correct mistakes

ARE YOU A GOOD CREDIT RISK?

No-one has a right to credit. Before giving you credit, lenders - such as banks, loan companies and shops - want to check whether you are an acceptable risk.

Credit reference agencies

To help them do this, they may check with firms called **credit reference agencies** to get some basic details about you and your credit record.

The main credit reference agencies keep information on their computers about almost every adult in the United Kingdom.

These agencies do not keep 'blacklists', or give any opinion about whether or not you should be given credit. They just provide information about your credit record. The lender decides whether you are an acceptable risk.

Credit scoring

Many lenders use credit scoring systems which allocate points to various pieces of information given on your application form, such as your age, your occupation and whether you own your home. These points are added together to produce your **credit score**. This helps the lender predict whether you are an acceptable risk.

Fig. 5.1.8 The Office of Fair Trading's series Know Your Rights *includes a useful booklet on* Credit Reference Agencies

Providing the facts contained on the file are accurate, there is nothing you can do to amend the records. If the entry is incorrect, then you can ask the agency to change it. These are the steps to follow:

• write to the CRA and ask them to remove or change the entry (they have to reply within 28 days)

• if the agency does not reply, then you can send a *notice of correction*. This needs to be sent within 28 days. This notice can be up to 200 words long

• if the agency amends or adds to your file, then

it must send on these details to anyone who has asked about you in the past six months

- if the agency does not reply to the letter enclosing the notice of correction within 28 days, then the Director-General of Fair Trading can be asked to intervene
- you need to give your full name and address, and that of the CRA. Along with this should be the details of the incorrect entry, stating why it is incorrect and why you will suffer if it is not changed. You also need to include the date on which you sent the notice of correction to the agency
- the Director-General will now ask the CRA to comment. You will be sent a copy of the reply. The Director-General will decide on how the matter will need to be resolved

Restrictions (use of exclusion clauses, other contractual terms)

Under the Unfair Contract Terms Act 1977 (particularly sections 6 and 7), there are a number of controls to limit contract terms which are designed to exclude or limit liability. Section 6 of the Act specifically covers the sale of goods and hire purchase agreements. Section 7 looks at all other contracts which involve situations when the ownership of goods passes from one person to another. In fact, both sections contain very similar information and rules.

In cases when the customer is a consumer or member of the public, there cannot be any exclusion of terms implied under the Sale of Goods Act 1979 (sections 12–15). This also extends to the provisions in the Supply of Goods (Implied Terms) Act 1973, as well as the Supply of Goods and Services Act 1982. In other words, the consumer has a great deal of protection.

In situations when the customer is not a consumer (in other words the goods were not purchased for personal or private use but were bought by a business), there can also be no exclusion of liability for breaches in implied terms that relate to the title of the product.

When the contract relates to hiring, there can be exclusions in the implied terms that relate to the supplier's right to transfer the ownership of the goods. This is fairly obvious since the whole purpose of hiring goods is not to obtain ownership.

The court has some tricky problems in determining whether exclusion clauses are reasonable. Some factors which they may wish to take into account include:

- the bargaining strength of either party
- whether the product is available elsewhere without these exclusion clauses
- whether the buyer was offered an incentive to accept the clause
- whether the goods were manufactured to the buyer's specification or design
- whether the customer should have reasonably known about the exclusion clause

Many of the exclusion clauses are invalidated under the Unfair Contract Terms Act 1977. This means that they cannot be used as the defence if a customer starts an action for damages. It should be remembered that this Act does not stop a supplier from using invalid clauses, but they have no legal standing. The problem is, of course, that many consumers are misled as they have little legal understanding. The Consumer Transactions (Restrictions on Statements) Orders 1976 and 1978 attempt to stop this unfair practice in certain situations. For our purposes, it means that a trader cannot attempt to exclude their liability in sections 13–15 of the Sale of Goods Act 1979. It is, in fact, a criminal offence if they do so. Specifically, they must not:

- display notices in places where consumers are likely to purchase the product
- include the clause in any of their advertisements
- provide or offer a consumer a contract with these clauses in them
- attempt to include a clause which denies liability with respect to quality or fitness for purpose

Focus study
Fair contracts

Consumers gained unprecedented powers to challenge the fairness of contracts attached to every product and service they buy, including insurance, bank accounts, holidays and mobile phones.

The Unfair Terms in Consumer Contract Regulations, viewed as the most sweeping consumer-rights law ever introduced in the UK, effectively give the consumer the benefit of the doubt in most disputes. Any contract weighted *unfairly* against the consumer will be deemed invalid under the new law.

Under the new rules, based on a European Directive, consumers can contest any contract they believe to be unfair. An action can be brought through the courts or the Office of Fair Trading.

The new law goes much further than the existing Unfair Contracts Terms Act of 1977. It demands not only fairness but also that plain English be used in contracts. It embraces insurance companies for the first time, compelling them to issue policies in *intelligible language* or risk having to rewrite whole contracts in the customer's favour. Also, any policy contract printed in tiny, unreadable type or written in gobbledegook, regardless of the *fairness* of its content, could be deemed *unfair*.

Insurance companies have rushed to redraft their contracts. Some insurers have even sought approval for their new terms from the Plain English Society.

Travel insurance may also have to be revised. The National Consumer Council states that: 'Many travel policies cover money stolen from your money belt, not money stolen from your bedside table.'

Insurers may also lose their right to impose more than one excess clause, where the policyholder is unfairly forced to pay the first few hundred pounds of *several items* within *one claim*.

Clauses that impose a time limit on claims and demands for policyholders to notify the insurer immediately of any alterations in risk are likely to be challenged too.

Banks and building societies also fear a consumer backlash. The British Bankers Association and the Building Societies Association have urged their members to redraft contracts to pre-empt disputes. Consumer lawyers agree that contracts that allow banks to switch funds between accounts, close accounts or raise charges without the customers' consent would be deemed unfair.

Travel companies seem less bothered by the new law, despite their vulnerability. Thomas Cook, the travel agent, said that existing codes of conduct covered the travel industry. But tour operators that change hotels at the last moment, or charge high penalties for cancellation, are likely to be told to compensate customers and rewrite their contracts.

Contracts expected to be deemed *unfair* proliferate across other industries: estate agents would no longer be able to hide behind contracts freeing them from liability for faulty or damaged holiday lettings; mobile-phone operators would not be able to shut down services at short notice; and makers of burglar alarms would no longer be able to deny liability for faulty products. Manufacturers' guarantees and rental and leasing agreements will also come under scrutiny.

▼

Focus study
Holidays and the
consumer

Tour operators' brochures should contain comprehensive and accurate details on the following:

- price
- destination
- transport
- itineraries
- accommodation
- meals provided
- visa/passport requirements
- health formalities
- amount of advance payment required
- whether the holiday is dependent on a minimum number of people booking

Probably the safest thing to do is to book through agents or operators who belong to a bonding scheme. These include:

- The Association of British Tour Agents (ABTA)
- The Association of Independent Tour Operators (AITO)
- The Federation of Tour Operators (FTO)
- The Association of Bonded Travel Organisers Trust (ABTOT)
- The Confederation of Passenger Transport UK
- The Passenger Shipping Association (PSA)

Tour operators must have an Air Transport Organisers Licence (ATOL).

Fig. 5.1.9 Package Holidays in the Single Market *produced by the Consumers in Europe Group, an umbrella body for UK organisations with an interest in the effects of European Union policies on UK customers, provides useful hints and tips on handling holiday problems*

The recommended way of dealing with problems when you are on holiday is:

- contact the company's local representative or the company directly
- contact a local tourist office or consumer advice agency for additional help
- make sure that you have the full details, and write to the company as soon as you get back from holiday
- any photographs or supporting evidence will be helpful too
- if the problem is not resolved then you should consider taking legal action
- the Citizens' Advice Bureau or trading standards office will be able to advise you on your rights
- ABTA offers an arbitration scheme, and this can be pursued, but you should remember that

if you are not successful then you cannot take legal action
- AITO also offers an independent dispute settlement service (provided the holiday was operated by one of their 148 members)
- the Trading Standards Offices may also be able to investigate and take appropriate action

Compensation under product liability law

There is a duty of general care which suppliers must have towards their customers. They must not offer goods which may result in an injury to the consumer's life or property. In other words, they have a duty of care to their customers. Perhaps the key word in all of this is *manufacturer*. In regard to product liability, this includes everyone who was involved from the design of the product to its final distribution. It also includes all of those who have been remotely involved with the product at any time.

In other words, defects in the product may give rise to liability. The manufacturer and distributor, and indeed anyone else involved in the product at all, needs to be assured that the products are examined from time to time to ensure that defects have not arisen.

The *duty of care* is owed to the ultimate consumer, and this also includes anyone using or consuming the product, regardless of whether they were the person who purchased the product in the first place.

Court judgements have shown that the *duty of care* is towards any injury, life or property. So this will include death, personal injury and damage to property, but it does not include damage to the product itself. One tricky area is any financial loss which is suffered as a result of the product failing to perform correctly.

Once the manufacturer has failed to exercise a *duty of care*, then the plaintiff needs to show that there is an element of *negligence liability*. The breach of duty shows that the manufacturer did not take reasonable care and this is the manufacturer's fault. The plaintiff would have to use witnesses who can show that the procedures or processes used by the manufacturer indicate a lack of care.

The Latin term *res ipsa loquitur* which means *the thing speaks for itself*, is a claim that can be made by the plaintiff. In these cases the manufacturer needs to satisfy the court that any injury or loss was not caused by their negligence. It is not sufficient in most cases for the manufacturer to show that they have a comprehensive quality control system and that the employees are well supervised. The manufacturer must attempt to make sure that they are prepared for possible and foreseeable misuses of their product. This means that the manufacturer has a very high standard of care imposed upon them by law.

The Consumer Protection Act 1987 was introduced partly in response to the EC directive on product liability (85/374/EEC). This introduced a significant extension to consumer protection with regard to the liability for injury caused by defective products. In order to prove liability under section 2 of the Act, which covers damage caused wholly or partly by a defective product, the plaintiff will need to prove the following:

- that the product was in fact defective
- that it was the defect that caused the injury or damage

Liability can, as we have seen, be attributed to a number of different organisations or individuals. For more information on this area, please refer to the section on product liability in 5.1.2 of this Element.

Proving that an injury was caused by a defect often rests upon showing that, under normal circumstances, the user of that product would expect it to be safe. Again, as we have said in 5.1.2, the user should expect the product to be generally safe in most situations. In this respect the packaging or labelling on a product should point out any particular circumstances when the product should not be used.

The defences against liability for defective products have been looked at in section 5.1.2 and are covered in full in section 4 of the Consumer Protection Act.

In part 2 of the Consumer Protection Act 1987, it points out that it is a criminal offence to supply goods to the consumer which are unsafe. Remember that this only refers to consumer goods.

In pairs, discuss your solutions to the following cases:

a young man was walking along the road when the wheel of a lorry broke free and hit him. The vehicle had been recently serviced by a garage. Who can be sued by the pedestrian?

a chemicals company supplies chemicals for industrial use. Unfortunately, he chemical exploded on contact with water. What type of negligence is this?

5.1.4 EXPLAIN THE TYPES OF LEGAL ACTIONS WHICH MAY RESULT FROM NON-COMPLIANCE WITH CONSUMER LAW

TYPES OF LEGAL ACTIONS

This can be extremely complicated, but you will need to know which types of proceedings a particular action may give rise to. In unfair dismissal cases, they will be heard by Industrial Tribunal. If the organisation has breached the contract of employment, then they may be sued in the county or high court. You will need to understand the process of bringing the action to the relevant court, the actual hearing of the case and the outcome. In Health and Safety cases an organisation may be prosecuted under the Factories Act 1961, or an injured employee may sue the organisation in the civil court for negligence.

In many cases, simply stating that you intend to take the matter to court will result in the complaint being sorted out. If it is necessary to take the organisation to court, it is often much easier than you would think and is often worth all the effort.

If the trader is a member of a trade association, there may be what is called *a conciliation or arbitration scheme* available. These schemes are informal and quite cheap. Sometimes, however, arbitration is not as cheap as going to court using the small claims procedures. The idea behind *arbitration and conciliation* is that both parties settle the differences between themselves. This is not a legally binding decision, and if you are unsatisfied with the outcome of the arbitration then you can go on to court. Both sides put their cases forward and the arbitrator makes a decision. The arbitrator may be a member of the Chartered Institute of Arbitrators. Arbitration is sometimes undertaken in writing, so, if you really want to put your case in person, then it may be better to go to the small claims court.

It is always a good idea to seek advice before going into arbitration or going to court. Some solicitors will work in law centres or advice agencies and not charge for their advice. In private practice a solicitor may be able to offer a low-cost interview. In all cases, the Citizens Advice Bureau will be able to help you find the right solicitor to meet your needs.

Criminal and civil

There are a variety of courts in the UK. They are principally split into either *civil* or *criminal courts*. The *civil courts* include the *county courts* and the *high court*. Nearly all of the proceedings take place in these courts. The *criminal courts* include the *magistrates' courts* and the *crown courts*.

The *county courts* are mainly involved in recovering money. There may be situations when there is a breach of contract between the customer and the business (in this sense the business may be a debtor as they have not given you the service or product agreed). Claims for damages, trespass and negligence are also heard in these courts. The maximum size of the case that can be heard in a *county court* is £50,000.

When claiming for money to be returned or for compensation, the case begins with a *default summons*. This is for either a fixed amount or an unfixed amount. Cases or actions that do not involve money are started with a *fixed date summons*. These cases usually involve disputes.

Perhaps the most common form of case that relates to consumer law is the *small claim*. These are used in cases when there has been a breach of contract, or where a small debt needs to be recovered. *Small claims courts* do not exist as such, but they are often referred to as this. The systems behind *small claims procedures* are fairly simple, but should the case become complicated then it can be referred back to the main civil system. *Small claims* can be made for up to £1,000, and within this you can include both the actual loss and the additional losses related to the problem. If, for example, your central heating engineer failed to repair your system properly, you could include the cost of hiring calor gas fires to keep your house warm.

The procedures are straightforward:

- you should first send a letter marked *final letter before action*. This should state that you intend to begin court proceedings. This is important as you may have to claim court fees and interest in the future. In most cases the debtor will now settle

- make sure that you know who the debtor actually is. This means that you need a name to sue. You can, of course, sue more than one person under the same case. Make sure that this is stated when beginning the proceedings. This also goes for businesses, organisations and authorities. You do not have to serve the summons at the registered address: any of the premises that the business uses will do

- make sure that you have collected all the relevant forms from the county court. All of these forms have the letter 'N' on them. You must use the right forms, and you will need three copies, one for yourself, one for the court and one for the court to send to the person or organisation you are suing. It is acceptable to send photocopies

- when you do issue a summons, you will have to pay a fee. The amount will depend upon the amount of your claim. Remember that you will get this back if you win. You can then take or send the form to the court

- the summons is then served on the defendant. Under normal circumstances this is done by post by the court. If the defendant is hard to find, then you can use bailiffs to serve the summons (this will cost you an extra £10)

- the debtor now has a choice. Either they can pay in full within 14 days, admit the claim is valid and offer a schedule of payments, or deny the claim and bring their own counter-claim

If at this point the summons is defended and your claim is for £1,000 or less, the claim will be referred to arbitration. If it is for more than £1,000, it can still go to arbitration or to court.

If it is not defended then you can apply to the court to have a judgement made. This is known as a *judgement in default*. This means that you can request that the payment be made now. You will have to fill in more forms though, and if it is complicated, the case now goes to trial.

The majority of small claims are referred to the defendant's court. This means that you will have to travel to their court. You can ask for the trial to be heard at your local court, but you will need to put this in writing and send it to the District Judge.

You will be given 14 days' notice before the hearing. This gives both sides time to swap documents and organise their witnesses.

At this stage you will have to make sure that you have got all your evidence sorted out. Remember that if the case has gone as far as a hearing, the defendant thinks that they are in the right too. You will have to prove that you are right on the *balance of probabilities*. This is somewhat different from criminal cases, where it has to be proved *beyond reasonable doubt* that one side is the guilty party.

The hearings themselves will take place between 10 and 4 on week days. They will only usually take around 1–2 hours. The judgement is known as *an award*. If you win then you will get the costs and the expenses included. To this will be added the debt.

If you lose, you can appeal, but only on a point of law or if you can prove that there was prejudice or misconduct involved.

In a large number of cases one of the main problems at this stage is the fact that the debtor does not have any assets. In order to enforce the payment of the debt, one of the following steps can be taken:

- a *warrant of execution* – this means that the debtor's goods can be seized and sold to cover the amount of the judgement plus the costs of the execution. In order to do this you will need to fill in a *request for warrant of execution* to allow the bailiff to seize the goods
- a *charging order* – which normally relates to land and in which case the debtor cannot dispose of property or stock and receive the full value of it before paying you
- a *garnishee order* – which means that if the debtor is owed money by a third party, then this money is transferred directly to you
- an *attachment of earnings* – this is an order which means that the debt is deducted from the employee's wages and is obviously not useful if the debtor is self-employed
- *appointment of receiver by way of equitable execution* – this is really the last course of action. The court will need to appoint a receiver who will get payment from the assets which are detailed in that order. This may include money from joint accounts and insurance policies

Having looked at the civil side of the law, we will now turn our attention to the criminal offences. To be a crime, an offence has to have been committed against a particular person. Normally, investigations are begun by the police. If they think that they have got sufficient evidence they will refer the matter to the Crown Prosecution Service (CPS). The CPS makes the final decision whether or not to prosecute. Around 95 per cent of all criminal cases are heard in the magistrates' courts. These cases are heard by the 30,000 lay-justices, and they have a range of sentencing powers. Their limits are fines of up to £5,000 and sentences of up to six months. They can, of course, make other conditions or discharges, or impose community or probation orders. Most appeals go onto the crown court and are heard by a judge and jury.

NON-COMPLIANCE

Contractual and negligence

As we have already shown earlier in this element, non-compliance either contractually or in terms of negligence can involve civil or even criminal proceedings. Most of the criminal consumer law is enforced by local authorities by their trading standards, consumer protection or customer services departments. In cases which involve hygiene, this is the responsibility of the environmental health departments. Broadly speaking, the following organisations are responsible for the various complaints or potential actions:

- complaints about business names – trading standards
- complaints about credit – trading standards
- complaints about dangerous goods – trading standards
- descriptions of products and advertisements – trading standards or Independent Broadcasting Authority, or, in certain cases, Office of Fair Trading
- unhygienic food or dirty premises – environmental health
- door-to-door salesmen – the police
- estate agents – trading standards and Office of Fair Trading
- fair trading and competition – Office of Fair Trading
- fraud and theft – the police
- guarantees – trading standards
- hallmarking – trading standards or the hallmarking council
- insurance – ombudsmen or self-regulating organisation
- prices – trading standards or Department of Trade and Industry (DTI)
- short weights or measures – trading standards
- unsolicited goods – trading standards

Referring specifically to non-compliance with *contractual aspects*, the following should be borne in mind:

- the seller is always liable, but the seller may be able to claim indemnity from the previous seller in the chain of distribution
- the buyer is the only one who can claim
- the liability is strict and refers to goods which are not reasonably fit for usual or notified special purposes
- the types of loss included relate to personal in-

jury, death, damage to property and financial loss
- there is no exclusion of liability, if the buyer is a consumer, in respect of death or personal injury
- in the case of personal injury, the claimant must make the claim within three years

Referring specifically to non-compliance in respect of *negligence*, the following should be borne in mind:

- the manufacturer, designer or repairer and, indeed, anyone else who has worked on the goods is liable
- the consumer is the only person who can make a claim
- liability is based on a fault which infers a failure to take reasonable care
- types of losses include personal injury, death, damage to property and, in some cases, financial loss
- exclusion of liability is prohibited if the negligence has resulted in death or personal injury
- the time limit for claims are three years from the date of the claimant being in possession of the fact that a negligent act was committed

▼

Focus study
Direct Selling
Association

The members of the Direct Selling Association (DSA) are involved in door-to-door and party-plan selling. Their Code of Practice not only guarantees everything that they sell, but also gives you the right to cancel your order within 14 days. Complaints are handled by their independent code administrator.

assignment

In order to cover the minimum requirements of these performance criteria, you will have to make a summary of the consumer rights which we have outlined in this element. Each of the tasks refer to specific performance criteria. You should produce your information in the form of a booklet.

TASK **1** PC 5.1.1

Explain the main objectives of consumer law.

TASK **2** PC 5.1.2

Describe the areas of the consumer protection legislation.

TASK **3** PC 5.1.3

Explain the rights of consumers in relation to the consumer protection legislation.

TASK **4** PC 5.1.4

Explain the different types of legal action that could result from an organisation's non-compliance with consumer law.

NOTES

This element and the assignment extends the information that you have been given in Unit 3 Consumers and Customers. You will have to be aware of all the main pieces of legislation that relate to consumer protection.

Your tutor will be able to help you collect information from the local consumer protection organisations where you will find a wide variety of leaflets and booklets to help you.

Explain the Role of Consumer Organisations in Providing Consumer Protection

Performance criteria

A student must:

1 explain the **role** of **consumer organisations**
2 identify and give examples of the **services** provided by one **consumer organisation**
3 describe the **features** of Citizen's Charter initiatives

RANGE

Role: advisory, regulatory, promotional, investigatory, lobbying, local, national, public sector, private sector

Consumer organisations: Citizens' Advice Bureau (CAB); Consumers' Association, National Consumer Council, Ombudsmen; trading standards, utility regulators

Services: advice, information, representation

Features: content, purpose, rights, protection, remedies

5.2.1 EXPLAIN THE ROLE OF CONSUMER ORGANISATIONS

ROLE OF CONSUMER ORGANISATIONS

Each of the different consumer organisations will have a series of aims and responsibilities. You will not need to know in any great detail how these organisations are structured. Neither will you need to remember their working arrangements, but you will have to investigate the arrangements to ensure *representative membership*; in other words, the arrangements that have been made to ensure that the organisation is both *representative* of the consumers and *independent* of any external influences or pressures.

Advisory

Business organisations are, perhaps, the most enduring and powerful advisory group. Obviously, the larger organisations are better placed to influence and advise government. Many of the larger organisations use professional lobbyists or have specific departments whose role it is to liaise with the various government departments, agencies and other organisations.

These activities are designed to make sure that the organisation's point of view is held in high regard by the government. In some cases, such as the debate on the banning of tobacco advertising, the businesses find themselves directly opposed to the policies of the government.

Through the various changes of commerce, employers' associations, the trade associations and the Confederation of British Industry, the views and interests of the business organisations have developed a strong voice.

Not only do the business organisations attempt to influence and advise the UK government, but they find themselves increasingly involved in attempts to influence the EU.

Focus study Confederation of British Industry

This organisation represents thousands of companies that employ literally millions of people. The members of the organisation are drawn from all the different sections of the economy and are both large and small businesses.

The organisation promotes the interests of the business community in general. It has regular contacts with both UK politicians and those that are involved with the European parliament.

It has been working closely with the UK government on environmental policies, for example. To this end, it has set up a policy unit which aims to:

- provide information
- offer contacts with MPs
- offer advice to MPs
- monitor developments in legislation
- liaise with government departments
- liaise with enforcement agencies
- lobby the government
- produce promotional materials
- organise conferences and seminars
- conduct surveys
- help members to develop good environmental management practices

Focus study The Institute of Plumbing

The Institute maintains a voluntary register of plumbers. The organisation dates back to the last century, requiring all registered plumbers to satisfy the Institute of their competence, experience, quality, workmanship and conduct.

The Institute will take action against a registered plumber if there are complaints by customers. The Institute of Plumbing's Business Directory of Registered Plumbers can be found in the following locations:

- public libraries
- Citizens' Advice Bureaux
- water companies
- regional gas consumer offices
- trading standards offices

The Institute also has a corporate advertisement in the Yellow Pages Directory.

Regulatory

In performance criteria 5.2.2 you will find a series of focus studies that cover some of the more well-known regulatory bodies. In this part of the element, we will look at the role of the Office of Fair Trading (OFT).

Fig. 5.2.1 *The Institute of Plumbing produce a leaflet which lays down guidelines for ensuring that the consumer always finds a competent plumber*

The OFT issue guidelines to help business in the following areas:

- what consumer and competition law requires of businesses
- the procedures any business must follow, and what happens if it fails to follow them
- the information that the OFT needs from businesses to pursue their statutory duties

The OFT are committed to observing the Code of Practice on Access to Government Information. They are well aware of the sensitiveness of the information that they receive from businesses. Their target time for responding to requests for information (under the Open Government Code) is just 20 days.

They are keen to keep in touch with the views of businesses, consumer organisations and enforcement bodies. To this end they:

- keep in touch with the business community through trade associations
- liaise with consumer organisations
- liaise with trading standards departments

Fig. 5.2.2 *The Office of Fair Trading's Citizen's Charter*

- consult businesses when changes in the law are being considered
- hold public hearings
- undertake customer surveys

The OFT is committed to being courteous and helpful at all times, responding to complaints quickly and fairly. They try to keep the costs as low as possible, making their operations as efficient as possible.

The Director General of the OFT has a number of key enforcement powers. These are:

- *Consumer Credit* – under the Consumer Credit Act 1974:

  administration of the licensing system

  adjudication in cases regarding the issuing, renewal, variation, suspension and relocation of businesses

  resolving disputes about credit reference agencies

  superintending the working and enforcement of the Act

- *Estate Agency* – under the Estate Agents Act 1979:

  the issue of prohibition orders

  issuing orders against estate agents guilty of misconduct

  superintending the working and enforcement of the regulations

- *Restrictive Practices* – under the Restrictive Trade Practices Act 1976:

  to compile and maintain a public register of restrictive trading agreements

  to refer registrable agreements to the Restrictive Practices Court

- *Mergers* – under the Fair Trading Act 1973:

  to be aware of any merger that may have to be referred to the Monopolies and Mergers Commission

  to recommend to the Secretary of State for Trade and Industry the action that may need to be taken in relation to such a merger

- *Monopolies and anti-competitive practices* –

under the Fair Trading Act 1973 and the Competition Act 1980:

to review commercial activities with a view to detecting monopoly situations and anti-competitive practices

to investigate situations where monopoly power and empty competitive practices have occurred, and remedy the situation by obtaining assurances and undertakings from the businesses in question

- *Trading Practices* – under the Fair Trading Act 1973:

  to review commercial activities with a view to identifying practices that may affect the interests of the consumer

  to seek assurances from trades where practices are detrimental to consumers or break the law. In extreme cases the matter will be referred to the courts

The Advertising Standards Authority (ASA) is the independent self-regulatory body responsible for supervising the content of non-broadcast advertisements in the UK.

It is estimated that there are some 25 million advertisements published annually in the UK. The ASA spot-checks thousands of them (and indeed sales promotions) as part of its rigorous monitoring programme.

The ASA also advises thousands of advertisers, agencies and publishers on how to avoid using misleading or offensive advertisements that may lead to complaints being made. The aim is *avoidance*, since complaints are not only costly but may involve adverse publicity and criticism of the industry.

The ASA operates on a levy charged on all advertisements. This levy, only 0.1 per cent of the advertisement's cost, is collected on the ASA's behalf by the Advertising Standards Board of Finance. This separation helps to ensure that the ASA maintains their independence.

The ASA has the power to investigate any complaint and compare the advertisement to the Code of Advertising Practice (see the next section of this element). The ASA rarely tells the advertiser to stop the advertisement immediately, as the advertiser is given the time to tell their side of the story.

If the advertisement is found to be unaccept-

WHAT DOES THE ADVERTISING STANDARDS AUTHORITY DO?

The ASA makes sure that advertising is legal, decent, honest and truthful.

The Authority safeguards the public by ensuring that the rules contained in the *British Code of Advertising Practice* are followed by everyone who prepares and publishes advertisements in the UK, and that advice is freely available to prevent problems arising. The Code lays down what is and is not acceptable in advertisements, except for those on television and radio.

It is estimated that more than 25 million advertisements are published in the UK each year. In addition to investigating complaints, the Authority also has a sophisticated and wide-ranging programme for monitoring advertisements to check that they observe the Code.

HOW CAN THE ASA STOP MISLEADING ADVERTISING?

The Authority uses the Code to decide what, if any, action needs to be taken. If an advertisement is unacceptable because it is misleading or in bad taste, the ASA will tell the advertiser to change or remove it.

The Authority seldom stops an advertisement immediately. Advertisers are usually given a limited time to tell their side of the story.

WHAT KIND OF ADVERTISEMENTS DOES THE ASA COVER?

The ASA is responsible for all advertisements in newspapers, magazines, posters, direct marketing, sales promotions, cinema, video cassettes and teletext (excluding ITV text services).

To comment on advertisements appearing on television or radio, which are not covered by the ASA, you should write to:

The Independent Television Commission
70 Brompton Road London SW3 1EY or

The Radio Authority 14 Great Queen Street
London WC2B 5DG

Complaints about claims made on packs or labels, with exception of the promotions described below, should be sent to your local Trading Standards or Environmental Health Officer, who can usually be contacted through your town hall or council offices.

The ASA can only deal with what is actually written or shown in an advertisement or in a promotion. It cannot take up other points where you disagree with a company's actions or where you are dissatisfied with a product or service. Ask at your Citizens' Advice Bureau or local advice centre where to complain.

WHAT ABOUT PROMOTIONS?

A promotion is generally a special offer of some kind such as a voucher, coupon, sample, prize promotion, competition, reduced price or free offer.

Sometimes the promotion is on the product pack, sometimes in a leaflet, or it may be in an advertisement.

Fig. 5.2.3 The ASA's complaints procedure

able under the rules of the Code, then the advertiser will be told to pull out the advertisement or amend it. Failure to do so will entail the advertiser being suspended; or suffering the withdrawal of privileges, with the publishers of magazines and newspapers being advised not to take their advertising.

Further refusal may entail the advertiser being referred to the OFT for refusing to abide by the Code. Under the Control of Misleading Advertisements Regulations (1988) the organisation can be restrained from using the advertisement ever again.

The ASA covers all advertisements in the following areas of the media and marketing activities:

- newspapers
- magazines
- posters
- direct marketing
- sales promotions
- cinema
- video cassettes
- teletext (not ITV)

Advertisements on TV and cable are covered by the Independent Television Commission (ITC). Radio is regulated by the Radio Authority.

Claims made on packets and labels are the preserve of the Trading Standards or Environmental Health Officers.

In conclusion, the ASA deals with only what is written or shown in an advertisement or a promotion. Complaints must be made in writing to the ASA with as much detail about the advertisement as possible (preferably a copy of the advertisement should be enclosed).

Focus study
Advertising
Standards
Authority

In March 1995, a much reported case was covered in the marketing press. It involved the advertising strategy of Colgate (run by Colgate Oral Care). It

was an example of *knocking copy*, which means that the advertisement openly criticised a competitor. Nothing particularly odd there, but it used one of their competitor's advertising slogans as part of its advertisement. It stated that Colgate's Plax mouthwash was approved by the British Dental Association (BDA) and that Listerine (owned by Warner Wellcome Consumer Healthcare) was approved *by a dragon called Clifford*. Quite amusing in its own right, but it was suggested that the advertisement had broken the British Code of Advertising Practice. Specifically, it states that:

> 'advertising should not make unfair use of the goodwill attached to the ... advertising campaign of any other business.'

Colgate also faces another problem from the ASA, in that the endorsement by the BDA incurs an annual fee. The ASA states that all financial relationships for product endorsements must be mentioned in the advertisement. This was not. Colgate, meanwhile, were confident that the advertisement was within the spirit and codes of the law.

Promotional

The Director-General of Fair Trading has powers under the Control of Misleading Advertisement Regulations 1988. He has the power to step in if the public interest requires that advertisements complained about need to be stopped by a court injunction.

The bulk of the complaints are handled by the following organisations:

- trading standards (or consumer protection) departments who enforce the Trade Descriptions Act and other consumer laws
- the Advertising Standards Authority who administer the British Code of Advertising Practice and the British Code of Sales Promotion Practice, in conjunction with the Code of Advertising Practice Committee

There are a number of other organisations, such as the Department of Health and Social Security, who have responsibilities concerning the Medicines Act.

Returning to the Director-General, he has power to cover the following types of advertisement:

- newspapers
- magazines
- outdoor advertising (buses, taxis, posters, etc.)
- cinema
- brochures, leaflets and visits
- point-of-sale materials
- display materials
- circulars and direct mail

The Director-General does not have responsibility for commercial television, radio or cable. These are covered by the following organisations:

- *The Independent Broadcasting Authority* – which has responsibility for all advertisements on ITV, Channel 4 and independent radio
- *The Cable Authority* – which has responsibility for all advertisements on licensed cable services

For further information on the operations of the Office of Fair Trading and how complaints are handled, please see the section on their operations earlier in this element.

Focus study
Mailing Preference Service

The Mailing Preference Service (MPS), set up in 1983, aims to establish good relations between direct mail issues and the general public.

The key aspects of the service are:

- to put aside the fears and misunderstandings that the public may have regarding direct mail
- to promote good practice
- to help individuals have their names removed from or added to mailing lists

Consumers purchase around £8 billion worth of products and services by post. Shopping from home is convenient, but, from time to time, we all get unwanted direct mail. The MPS will attempt to ensure that the public only receive correctly addressed and named direct mail, and, if requested,

Fig. 5.2.4 The Mailing Preference Service issues a short guide for the consumer

you can have your name removed from the mailing lists but it takes around three months for the materials to decrease in volume.

Investigation and Lobbying

The Consumers' Association (CA) offer an ideal example of exactly how the investigatory and lobbying process works.

Once the consumer research has been completed, which would involve carefully checking all the details, the organisation provides the facts to the consumer. It is not enough, however, to concentrate on the consumer. It is true that through consumer action, businesses and the government can be influenced. The CA, for example, seek to broaden their influence further.

Their long-term approach is to bring pressure to bear upon the individual businesses (particularly the larger ones), trade associations, professional associations, standards bodies, government departments and agencies.

By gaining publicity for the issue in question, the pressure group can at least make people begin to talk about the problem. Using contacts to ensure that the consumer's point of view is considered and heard, is the next step and one that can only be taken after many years of activity in the area.

Members of the CA's council management, staff and ordinary members represent the consumers on statutory and public bodies. They also make a valuable contribution to such organisations as the British Standards Institution (BSI).

All pressure groups in this area are committed to making information available to the consumer. Many of them have campaigns units whose job it is to take up the recommendations for change and improvement revealed by research.

Campaigning in this way costs a lot of money. So the pressure groups do sell their merchandise, charge membership fees and accept donations, if appropriate.

Typical of the many organisations involved in investigatory or lobbying activities, the CA are often involved in several campaigns at a time. Amongst those that would interest groups in the consumer protection are:

- safety standards
- labelling
- uncompetitive activities (monopolies, etc.)
- pollution
- improving the availability of information
- simplifying contracts
- simplifying activities such as house buying

Local and national

There are a number of different consumer organisations. Obviously the more well-known ones are national organisations, found in both the public and the private sector. Here is a list of organisations that fall into the *national* category:

- Advertising Standards Authority
- Air Transport Users Committee
- Association of British Chambers of Commerce
- Association of British Insurers
- Association of British Travel Agents
- Association of Mail Order Publishers
- Banking Ombudsman Bureaux

- British Electro-technical Approvals Board
- British Hallmarking Council
- British Standards Institution
- Building Societies Association
- Building Societies Ombudsman
- Cable Authority
- Central Transport Consultative Committee
- Commissioner for Local Administration
- Companies Registry (Companies House)
- Consumer Policy Committee
- Consumers' Association
- Department of Trade and Industry
- Electricity Consumers Council
- Gas Consumers Council
- General Medical Council
- Health Services Commissioner
- Independent Broadcasting Authority
- Institute of Consumer Advisors
- Institute of Trading Standards Administration
- Insurance Ombudsman Bureaux
- Law Society
- Mailing Preference Services
- Mail Order Publishers Association
- Monopoly and Mergers Commission
- National Association of Citizens' Advice Bureaux
- National Consumer Council
- National Pharmaceutical Association
- Office of Data Protection
- Office of Fair Trading
- Office of Telecommunications
- Post Office Users National Council
- Securities and Investments Board
- Solicitors Complaints Bureau

Locally, the organisations will tend to fall under the control or financing of the local authorities. These would include the trading standards offices and the environmental health departments.

Public sector

There are a number of public sector organisations that are charged with the responsibility of defending and legislating in favour of consumer rights. These organisations, primarily funded directly by the government (or, in some cases, via other means, such as local trading standards), cover all aspects of the area of consumer protection and legislation.

It is very easy to get confused about the different organisations that operate in the public sector. Here is a basic rule of thumb to help you understand:

- Some of the organisations are part of major central government departments
- Some of the organisations operate on behalf of central government departments; these are often known as QUANGOs (quasi-autonomous non-governmental organisations)
- Some of the organisations are financed by central government but are fairly independent of them
- Some organisations are fully independent, apart from a reliance on some or all funding from central government
- Some organisations are part of the local government structure and receive finance from them

Focus study
Environmental
health

Environmental health departments, which are part of the local authority's attempts to control various abuses which could be practised by businesses and other organisations, have a staggering amount of legislation to cover. A small proportion of the legislation is listed below:

- Animal Boarding Establishments Act 1963
- Animal Health Act 1981
- Animal Health and Welfare Act 1984
- Breeding of Dogs Act 1973
- Building Act 1984
- Caravan Sites and Control of Development Act 1960

LAND AND WATER

Our Brierley Court hop farms nurture the hedgerows so that flora and fauna may flourish

BRIERLEY Court Hop Farms have worked to a conservation plan since 1980.

The hedges are trimmed to encourage spring flowers and autumn berries to flourish as a natural habitat for wildlife and nearly 60 species of birds have been observed at the farm.

Callaway Vineyard & Winery in Temecula, California, is helping both the homeless and environment. Twelve hawk perch posts and twelve nesting boxes were erected to encourage wild birds to remain in the vineyard. Both the birds and Callaway benefit from this unique system.

The Callaway vineyards in California have provided a home for families of hawks

THE LEISURE ENVIRONMENT

IN OUR pubs and restaurants we provide a variety of attractive environments in which our customers may enjoy their leisure hours.

We have surveyed with considerable care the needs and wishes of our customers and wherever possible design our pubs to meet the needs of the area in which they operate.

We also sponsor the provision of litter bins and refuse collection and an increasing number of pubs with car parking facilities are donating space to the siting of bottle banks.

Sponsorship and fund-raising activities are widespread among our pubs and their efforts continue to play a major role in supporting the communities which they serve.

The addition of a few flowers can add visual appeal to pubs which already present an attractive face to the world

Fig. 5.2.5 Allied Domecq (formerly Allied Lyons) are keen to show that they have environmental health in mind and produce their booklet Good Environmental Practice

- Cinemas Act 1985
- Clean Air Acts 1956 and 1968
- Control of Pollution Act 1974
- Dangerous Wild Animals Act 1976
- Dogs Act 1906
- Fire Precautions Act 1971
- Food Act 1984
- Health and Safety At Work Act 1974 (plus 800 other regulations)
- Housing Act 1985
- Local Government (Miscellaneous Provisions) Acts 1976 and 1982
- Offices, Shops and Railway Premises Act 1963
- Pet Animals Act 1951
- Poisons Act 1972
- Prevention of Damage by Pests Act 1949
- Public Health Acts 1936 and 1961
- Public Health Control of Diseases Act 1984
- Rag, Flock and Other Filling Materials Act 1961
- Refuse Disposal (Amenity) Act 1978
- Riding Establishments Act 1964–1970
- Scrap Metal Dealers Act 1964
- Shops Act 1950
- Slaughter House Act 1974
- Water Act 1989
- Zoo Licensing Act 1981
- Fresh Meat Export (Hygiene and Inspections) Regulations 1987
- Meat Inspection Regulations 1987
- Meat (Sterilisation and Staining) Regulations 1982
- Poultry, Meat (Hygiene) Regulations 1994
- Slaughterhouses (Hygiene) Regulations 1977

Obviously, some of these pieces of legislation do not have immediate relevance to consumer protection. However, all of these laws are designed to ensure that the worst excesses of rogue businesses are controlled.

Private sector

Being a part of the private sector means that the organisation does not receive finance from central or local government with strings attached. In other words, private sector organisations, whether they are pressure groups, consumer interest groups, trade associations, or lobby specialists, all have an involvement in consumer protection but may not be wholly separate from

the government, that is, they may play an advisory role.

The public sector organisations tend to be either charities or limited companies, relying on membership fees or other forms of funding in order to continue their activities.

Maintaining their independence is vital not only to the organisation, in terms of giving it *freedom* to do as it wishes, but also to the consumer. Without freedom of action the organisations could never support or promote the rights and needs of the public.

5.2.2 IDENTIFY AND GIVE EXAMPLES OF THE SERVICES PROVIDED BY ONE CONSUMER ORGANISATION

CONSUMER ORGANISATIONS

In this performance criteria we will look at the main consumer organisations and identify the services which they offer the public. To this end the information for each of the organisations will follow a common format and address the following:

- advice
- information
- representation

We have attempted to use the latest information on each of these organisations, and have included examples of their work or action as appropriate.

Citizens' Advice Bureaux (CAB)

The Citizens' Advice Bureaux are funded by the local authorities and have a particular interest in the following:

- social security (pensions, benefits, national insurance)
- employment rights (unfair dismissal and tribunal procedures)

The consumer issues can usually be dealt with by telephone. For the most part the CAB will be able to help the enquirer access the information needed to pursue a grievance or problem.

There are over a thousand CAB outlets throughout this country. They are staffed by volunteers and paid employees and offer impartial, free and confidential advice.

The National Association of Citizens' Advice Bureaux (NACAB) cover England, Wales and Northern Ireland. This organisation monitors the types of complaint that the local bureaux handle. In some areas the CABs are known as Consumer Advice Centres.

Consumer Associations

The Consumers' Association (CA) came into existence to try and balance the power between the sellers and the buyers. Founded in 1957, it provides an independent guidance service to the consumer.

The Consumers' Association methodically tests and investigates the goods and services available to the consumer. They publish comparative reports which look at the following aspects of goods and services:

- their performance
- their quality
- their value

This information is published in the various *Which?* magazines.

In order to maintain their independence, the Consumers' Association state the following:

- they only serve the interests of the consumer
- they do not accept money from the government, trade or industry
- they have no advertising in their magazines
- they never accept free samples, holidays or meals

Fig. 5.2.6 *The Consumers' Association publish their findings in the* Which? *magazines*

Fig. 5.2.7 *The Consumers' Association has been based in Buckingham Street, London, for the last 26 years*

- they do not allow their findings or recommendations to be used by trade or industry to promote their products or services
- they are not politically motivated
- they do not allow practising business people to sit on their governing council

▼

Focus study Consumer associations

Consumer groups have recently started a new campaign against insurance policies and other contracts that use fine print to deny policyholders payments or impose unfair penalties. The Consumers' Association and the National Consumer Council (NCC) have encouraged consumers to send examples of unfair contracts to the Office of Fair Trading (OFT).

The OFT's response was that investors do not need to have bought a product to be eligible to complain. All they need to show is that the contract was unfair.

Under existing UK law, there is some protection under the Unfair Contract Terms Act 1977, although the insurance companies have been exempt. New legislation will ensure that the UK complies with European directives which cover contracts for all (or most) goods and services.

Time-share contracts are due to be covered under the new law, as are mortgages and package holidays. This will have a massive impact on the excessive cancellation penalties demanded by package holiday operators.

It is in the area of travel insurance that the bulk of the complaints have been made regarding contracts.

New European directives give the OFT the power to take legal action against organisations which issue contracts considered to be unfair. In order to monitor this, a special unit has been set up, but both the CA and the NCC feel that it may not have sufficient resources. To this end, the NCC support the notion that consumer groups ought to be able to challenge contracts on behalf of individuals.

Fig. 5.2.8 The Office of Fair Trading produce a booklet, Avoiding Holiday Hassles, *for consumers*

There have been cases in some insurance policies of sentences running up to 130 words. One particular example, using a 36-word sentence, using no commas, defined money as:

'current legal tender cheques money order postal orders current postage stamps (not being part of a collection) national insurance stamps savings stamps or certificates premium bonds travellers cheques travel tickets luncheon vouchers gift tokens and phone cards.'

National Consumer Council

The National Consumer Council (NCC) represents the wishes of the consumer to the following:

- the government
- the utilities
- the public services
- the business community

As well as its lobbying and pressure group activities, it also carries out extensive research and publishes findings and recommendations.

The NCC was set up in 1975 by the government. It is the Council's duty to insist that the interests of all consumers be taken into account.

Its major priority is in consumer education and in the development of a network of information and advice centres nationwide.

The NCC has no statutory powers and does not deal with individual consumer complaints. It is fully funded by the government but is an independent organisation. There are similar councils set up for Scotland, Wales and Northern Ireland.

Focus study
Thames Water

The UK's biggest water company recently cut its investment programme by £350 million. What has annoyed consumer organisations is that it will not be passing on these savings to its seven million customers.

This comes at a time when there is growing public anger about the huge rises in the water company's profits and director's salaries. These appear to be funded by massive rises in charges since privatisation. Thames Water's bills, for example, have risen by 50 per cent above inflation to an average of £162 per household since privatisation. At the same time, the salary of the current chairman Sir Robert Clarke has risen 154 per cent from £41,000 per year to a staggering £104,000 per year.

The utility regulator OFWAT (Office of Water Services) support the consumer group's feeling that the reduction in investment should be passed onto the customer via either improved services or lower bills.

The NCC state that there is a very strong case for reducing bills if big savings are being made.

In response to these statements, the Thames Customer Service Committee replied:

'the customer is financing the company's investment. If the investment is reduced, the customer should benefit.'

Focus study
British Telecom

In response to OFTEL's proposals that BT should be allowed to charge customers as much as it likes for line rentals, the National Consumer Council stated that they were deeply concerned and would watch BT's responses very carefully.

Some three million customers take advantage of BT's Low User Scheme. This is one customer in five, and it is suggested that these will be protected by a guarantee that charges would not rise above inflation.

Despite the fact that the UK's telecommunications services are the most open in the world, with over 190 companies, BT still control 85 per cent of all telecommunications traffic.

Mercury Communications have managed to gain a quarter of the international telephone traffic, but have only recruited 750,000 domestic users.

These proposed changes will probably accelerate the move from BT to their rivals.

Ombudsmen

Ombudsmen were set up to investigate complaints about government departments or public sector organisations. They cover the following:

- poor service
- bad administration
- abuses of power

There are quite a number of ombudsmen which now operate in both the public and private sectors.

In order to use the ombudsmen, you must firstly have written to the organisation that you wish to complain about. This gives them the opportunity to sort the problem out. The ombudsmen can be seen as a cheaper (i.e. free) alternative to taking the matter to court. In any case, they tend to act more quickly than the courts.

Ombudsmen have different amounts of power to make sure that the organisation complies with

Ombudsmen	Number of complaints		
	1981	1991	1993
Police Complaints Authority [England and Wales]	–	18,065	17,991
Commissioners for Local Administration	3,295	14,060	16,507
Banking Ombudsman	–	6,327	10,231
Building Societies Ombudsman	–	8,264	9,142
Insurance Ombudsman	1,517	4,334	8,133
Independent Commission for Police Complaints for Northern Ireland	–	2,530	2,419
Corporate Estate Agents Ombudsman	–	1,236	2,340
Pensions Ombudsman	–	2,186	2,179
Health Service Commissioners	686	990	1,384
Legal Services Ombudsman	–	1,248	1,235
Broadcasting Complaints Commission	114	1,048	1,049
Parliamentary Commissioner for administration	917	801	986
Northern Ireland Parliamentary Commissioner and Commissioner for Complaints	654	547	605
Scottish Legal Services Ombudsman	41	303	295
Investment Ombudsman	–	67	103
Total for Year	7,224	62,006	74,599

Source: *Ombudsmen concerned.*
Edition: 25 Published 1995.
Crown Copyright – Social Trends 1995

Table 5.2.1 The number of complaints received by ombudsmen in the UK in 1995

the proposed resolution of the complaint. Sometimes the ombudsmen can demand compensation from the organisation on behalf of the complainant.

The main features of the ombudsmen scheme are:

- they operate independently
- they investigate complaints
- they decide whether there has been unreasonable delay, neglect, inefficiency or some other failure
- the complainant has the right to continue the complaint into court if they are unhappy with the ombudsmen's findings
- they can make recommendations about improved procedures and services for the future

Focus study
Insurance
ombudsman

In 1995 the insurance ombudsman received 2,027 complaints about life policies and endowments, compared with around 1,000 complaints about both motor insurance and household insurance. He found against life insurance companies in 42 per cent of cases, compared with 35 per cent in the case of motor and 31 per cent in household insurance. But travel insurance companies lost half the claims they were contesting.

Valuations were a major cause of complaints when cars were written off. The ombudsman maintains that the valuation should reflect the market value of the car. This is not its second-hand value, but its replacement value.

Valuations were also a problem area when it came to household insurance – particularly with jewellery theft claims. Insurers frequently knock down claims, arguing that there is insufficient proof of value.

Travel insurance is another area increasingly seen by the watchdog as a problem black spot. Complaints frequently arise because travellers buy policies without knowing the exclusions.

Trading standards

The safety provisions of the Consumer Protection Act 1987 allow the trading standards officers of the local authorities the following rights in respect of the safety of goods (as we have seen in element 5.1):

- to make test purchases to check on the safety of the goods
- to enter and search premises to obtain information (in certain cases)
- to issue suspension notices which prohibit the suppliers from selling the goods which are believed to break the safety legislation
- to apply to the magistrates' court for an order which allows them to seize and destroy such goods

The local trading standards departments check the following on behalf of the consumer:

- the products meet safety requirements (with labels, warnings and instructions)
- the composition of food meets the legal standards (i.e. accurate food labels which are not misleading)
- the weighing and measuring equipment used by traders is accurate
- the quantity markings on food and other products are accurate
- price claims and descriptions are not misleading
- credit and hire agreements meet legal requirements

They do this by:

- advising manufacturers, retailers and service providers on how to comply with the various laws
- inspecting goods at all stages of the production and distribution chain
- monitoring advertisements, catalogues and brochures
- taking food samples for analysis
- investigating complaints made by the public and other businesses
- seizing dangerous and illegal goods to stop them from being sold
- prosecuting businesses if the trading standards advice has been ignored

In order to contact the trading standards department, the consumer may either ring, write a letter or call in personally. In special circumstances, the trading standards officers will visit you at home (if you are disabled or house-bound).

Utility regulators

When various publicly owned industries were sold to private individuals, there was a very real fear that the overriding concerns of these organisations would be purely profit-based. Given the fact that the majority of these industries are monopolies (i.e. they are the only organisation to offer this service in a particular area), they had to be controlled and watched.

Whatever your view about privatisation, the fact is that the old state monopolies have now become private ones, especially in the case of British Gas, British Telecom and the electricity companies.

Regulators were put in place to oversee their operations. Again, there are differing views about the effectiveness of these regulators. Many people feel that the consumer is not well enough protected. There have been huge profit rises, despite the fact that there has been a recession.

The key regulatory bodies are:

- *Office of Electricity* (OFFER) set up in 1990, which regulates the prices of regional electricity companies
- *Office of Gas Supply* (OFGAS) set up in 1986 to regulate the gas supplies to domestic users
- *Office of Telecommunications* (OFTEL) set up in 1984; it regulates BT, including line rentals, calls, licences and equipment
- *Office of Water* (OFWAT) set up in 1989 to regulate the supply of water and sewerage, as well as price increases

Focus study
Office of Water
Services (OFWAT)

OFWAT is a government department responsible for making sure that the water industry provides customers with a good-quality and efficient service at a fair price. It is independent of the industry itself and headed by a Director-General.

If an individual has a complaint about any of the following, then the matter should be taken up with the company in the first place, to give them an opportunity to put things right:

* billing errors
* methods of payment
* new connections
* interruptions to supply
* water quality
* meter installation
* debt and disconnection
* liability for repair
* flooding from sewers
* leakage from pipes
* low water pressure

Fig. 5.2.9 The Office of Water Services (OFWAT) logo

All of the water companies have procedures for handling customer complaints. This is laid out in their *Code of Practice for Customers*. If the company fails to reply to the complaint within 10 days, then the customer may be entitled to compensation under the *Guaranteed Standards Scheme*.

If the company has not resolved the complaint to the satisfaction of the customer, then one of the 10 regional Customer Service Committees (CSCs) will investigate the problem. If the complaint is found to be justified, then the company will be required to take appropriate action.

Focus study
British Gas

According to the annual report from OFGAS, the office of the gas-industry regulator, complaints and queries rose by more than a quarter last year to 2,318 incidents. Disconnections rose from 16,088 to 16,393, reversing the trend of previous years.

OFGAS blamed British Gas's restructuring for the surge of unrest. Prices and discounts for direct-debit customers were mostly to blame.

OFGAS decided that British Gas was entitled to offer the discounts, provided that customers were offered prices in line with the company's costs. British Gas has promised to introduce these lower charges later this year. Philip Hanne, field officer with the Gas Consumers' Council said the rise in complaints showed that many customers felt the discount scheme for monthly direct-debit customers was unfair.

The OFGAS report shows that the North Thames region had the highest number of complaints in 1995, followed by South Eastern and North Western. The Northern and Scottish regions registered the smallest number of complaints.

The company has been warned by the government that its Charter Mark is under review because of concern about slipping standards.

5.2.3 DESCRIBE THE FEATURES OF CITIZEN'S CHARTER INITIATIVES

FEATURES

In this performance criterion we will be looking at the purposes and protection given to consumers by the various Citizen's Charter initiatives. We will concentrate on the most important ones and consider their aims and responsibilities. In particular, we will consider the following aspects:

- the content of the initiatives
- purposes of the initiatives
- rights arising out of the initiatives for the consumer
- protection given to the consumer by the initiatives
- remedies to problems provided by the initiatives

Content

The Citizen's Charter covers the following types of institution or organisation:

- schools
- hospitals
- council housing
- police services
- courts
- prisons
- postal services
- tax offices
- benefit offices
- job centres
- railways
- roads
- central government
- local government
- gas
- electricity
- water
- telecommunications

The principal aim of the Citizen's Charter is to im-prove public services across the board. Through it, the consumers should get a better deal along with better choice. One of the key aspects is to increase the amount of competition. This, it is hoped, will mean that the consumer will get better value for money.

The Citizen's Charter will aim to set standards and publish them. In this way the consumer will have access to more information about the services and be able to have remedies if the standards are not met.

Let us have a look at some of the principal improvements that have been suggested:

health – patients now have a guaranteed maximum waiting time of two years for admission into hospital. Now, nine out of 10 patients are admitted within a year. In April 1993 this waiting period came down to 18 months for three main treatments (hips, knees and cataracts)

education – parents now have better and greater amounts of information about the decisions made regarding their children. All parents receive a written report on their children at least once a year. Performance tables are now produced to cover the following:

- examination results
- truancy rates
- national curriculum test results
- information about school leavers
- summaries of the independent reports

British Rail – BR has to publish details on the punctuality and reliability of each line. The Charter also introduced two compensation schemes which give compensation if performance, or the number of delays, are above the published levels

council services – local councils are now obliged to tell their residents how they are performing. The Audit Commission publishes tables showing how the different councils compare

housing – the Housing and Urban Development Bill aims to introduce competition into local authority housing management. Tenants, for example, now have

46

	Chartermark	BS5750	Investors in People	UK Quality Award	Benefits Agency Quality Award	Golden Helix Award
Award body	Citizen's Charter Unit	BSI plus 30 other bodies	TECS	British Quality Foundation	Benefits Agency	Hewlett Packard
Number awarded per year	Up to 100	No limit	No limit	Few	Few	One
How long held	3 years	As long as organisation complies with standards	Three years	One year	Three years	One year
Eligibility	Public sector and regulated private utilities	Public/private sector	Public/private sector	Private, profit making	Units within the Benefits Agency	Healthcare organisations
Criteria for award	Nine criteria based on principles of public service	20 standard requirements	24 assessment indictors	Eight broad criteria	12 procedural requirements	Measurable quality improvements in customer service
Application process	Written, no longer than 10 pages	Submission of a quality manual	Submission of an action plan	Written submission no longer than 75 pages	Written self-assessment	Self-assessment and an improvement plan.
Cost of application	No charge	From £990	Usually paid by a TEC grant	£500–£1,500	No charge	No charge
Judging process	Panel/visits	Three-day visit	Visit	Panel/visits	Panel	Panel
Form of award	Trophy/certificate	Certificate/trophy	Plaque/certificate	Trophy/certificate	Plaque/certificate	£4,000–£5,000

Table 1.3.3 The different awards and how they are judged and awarded

the right to have their houses repaired quickly and efficiently

roads – road and highway authorities have a legal duty to tell the public why they are digging up the roads. They are also meant to control the times when the road works are in operation to avoid traffic chaos. As far as the motorways are concerned, new laws allow developers to build more service stations to improve the choice and competition in most stretches of motorway

Purpose

The main purpose of the Citizen's Charter is best summed up by the principles published in 1992. It laid out the following:

standards – to set, monitor and publish clear standards of service that the public should expect. To publish the actual performance against the standards for comparison

information and openness – to ensure that full, accurate information is readily available in a way in which all the public can understand. This information should show how the public services are run, what they cost, how they perform and who is in charge of them

choice and consultation – to ensure that courteous and helpful service is given by all public servants. They should always wear badges so that the individuals can be identified. It should also be ensured that all services are available on an equal basis and are run so that the public can have maximum access

putting things right – if things do go wrong, then the public service should apologise and give a full explanation, along with a quick and effective remedy. There should also be a well-publicised complaints procedure that is subject to independent review from time to time

value for money – to ensure that the public receives efficient and economical delivery of public services within the resources available. All services performance should be measured against published standards

Focus study Post Office Counters Ltd

The Post Office's Customer Charter, outlined in *Our Customer Charter*, identifies key areas for improvement or close consideration:

- *quick service* – ensuring that customers only have to wait a maximum of five minutes
- *personal service* – ensuring that the staff are attentive and courteous (they also wear name badges)
- *professional service* – involving well-trained staff that can give help and advice
- *information* – they aim to never run out of forms or leaflets. If they do, they will post them to the customer free of charge
- *complaints* – if the customer has a problem or a query, the manager or sub-postmaster should deal with the situation on the spot. Alternatively, if this is not acceptable, then a letter should be sent

Around 28 million customers visit the 20,000 Post Office outlets every week. Independent surveys and reports show that the queues are shorter than most banks, building societies, DIY stores and supermarkets.

The outlets offer a staggering 160 different services; this is far more than the majority of banks.

Rights

Despite the intentions of the Customer Charter, many people think that they are still receiving a pretty poor deal from the public services.

The Customer Charter promises better services from the NHS, schools, courts, benefit offices and other government organisations. Not only that, it also offers cash refunds for bad service from British Telecom, British Gas, the Post Office and British Rail.

It is true that, to date, there have been some improvements:

- hospital waiting lists are down

Fig. 5.2.10 The Post Office Customer Charter

- parents receive a school report
- court delays have been cut
- benefit payments have been speeded up
- driving tests can now be booked by telephone and paid for by credit card
- the waiting time has been reduced from 13 weeks to 5 weeks for a driving test

Despite all that, the cash refund side of the Customer Charter has all but failed. With the exceptions of OFTEL and OFGAS cutting the phone and gas bills, it appears to have had little effect on, for example, British Rail. Despite refund payments for around £10 million–£15 million per year, British Rail are incredibly slow in making these payments. British Rail's problem is that the Passengers Charter states that 90 per cent of the trains should arrive within five minutes of the published time. In fact, some routes can only achieve around 66 per cent. With season ticket holders entitled to 5 per cent rebate for late trains, and another 5 per cent if the train is cancelled, BR has a real problem.

Putting the rights of the public aside, BR has asked the government to lower the targets!

Protection

By late 1993 the amount paid to phone users who had cause to complain to BT had risen to £16 million. This is some £43,000 per day, but the fact of the matter is that the public cannot get anyone else except BT to mend their telephones. How else can an acceptable level of service be guaranteed? It does assume that BT will do their best, otherwise they will have to pay for not getting it right.

Perhaps the most famous private section pledge which protects the customer and assures an excellent level of service is that offered by Domino's, the pizza delivery service. Their pledge, '30 minutes or free', gives the customer confidence, as well as being able to create a sense of responsibility from the employees. Unfortunately, this pledge has backfired on the company, with allegations in the newspapers of their delivery vans and bikes being driven dangerously fast. This suggestion was, in fact, wrong, but the damage had already been done.

Protection of this sort has become more common. National Breakdown offer to pay £10 if they take more than one hour to arrive if you need to use their car rescue service. Rover will give you your money back if you are unhappy with one of their new cars. Books Etc. will refund the cost of the book you have purchased if you do not like the story.

In other public sector areas, such as local government, new initiatives offer protection too. Edinburgh District Council will refund £30 for enquiries about planning permission, building warrants, or completion certificates, if the request is not dealt with after one week. Their sports facilities will give the public a free booking as compensation if they find that their court or pitch is double-booked.

In the long term, protection such as this may well extend to theatres, cinemas and concert halls when the performance is late or the acoustics are poor.

Returning to BT, the typical protection schemes that can mean the customer will get compensation are:

* if a broken line is not mended by midnight the next day
* if an appointment is missed
* if a customer is disconnected by mistake

Payment is usually credited to the next bill, or if requested, the payment will be made by cheque, with a covering letter.

Remedies

In 1993, the government produced a booklet called *The Citizen's Charter Complaints Taskforce – Effective Complaining Systems*. This laid down the basic principles and checklists to be used.

The complaints system needed to be:

* accessible
* easy to understand
* able to provide an effective response
* independently reviewed

Complaints should be seen as a positive feedback method that can provide valuable information about weaknesses. Complaints allow the organisation to take action and improve standards of service.

The principles of the complaints system are:

* to be accessible and well-publicised
* to be simple to understand and use
* to be handled speedily with well-established limits for action
* to keep the complainant well informed
* to ensure a full and fair investigation
* to respect the complainant's desire for confidentiality (if applicable)
* to address all of the points raised and provide an effective response and appropriate redress
* to provide information to the management of the service so that the service can be improved

It also lays down a number of thoughts in the form of a checklist. These thoughts could well be used in other areas and for other organisations too:

* access to the complaints procedure
* handling of the complaint
* the outcomes of the complaint

assignment

Having looked at a variety of different consumer organisations, you must now investigate one of these in depth. In order to fulfil the performance criteria, you should tackle each of the tasks and prepare an oral presentation to your tutor and the rest of your group.

TASK **1** PC 5.2.1

Explain the role of one consumer organisation that provides consumer protection.

TASK **2** PC 5.2.2

Identify, with examples, the services provided by the consumer organisation.

TASK **3** PC 5.2.3

Describe the features of the Citizens Charter initiatives that refer to the organisation

NOTES

Good sources of information will induce

- employees/personnel of the organisation
- local authority departments
- local trading standards offices

Examine the Effects of Consumerism on the Provision of Products and Services

Performance criteria

A student must:

1 explain **reasons** for the growth of consumerism
2 explain the **purposes** of consumerism in relation to the provision of the products and services
3 suggest how consumerism **benefits business organisations**

RANGE

Reasons: pressure groups, untrue claims by business organisations, dangerous products, unreliable services

Purposes: defence of consumer interests, increase consumer influence, improve products, improve services, quality standards

Benefits: in terms of: unsolicited feedback from consumers, basis for modification (of products, of services), mutual understanding

Business organisations: private sector, public sector; large, medium, small

5.3.1 EXPLAIN REASONS FOR THE GROWTH OF CONSUMERISM

Consumerism is a term used to describe the general movement whose aim it is to influence the decisions of organisations in terms of their business activities. The pressure is on suppliers, manufacturers and distributors to make sure that their products are not dangerous or unreliable. The pressure even goes as far as to attempt to make sure that advertising and marketing activities stay within the limits of truth and reliability.

Although we will quickly look at some of the background behind the movement, our main focus will be upon recent developments.

It is worth noting that consumerism is far more common in countries that have developed economies, like the majority of Europe and the USA. With added choice and organisations competing for custom, businesses are keen to respond to the needs and demands of their customers.

REASONS FOR THE GROWTH IN CONSUMERISM

Many experts believe that the main reason for the growth in consumerism was the emergence of various media communications. The producers and manufacturers of consumer products need to be able to consistently sell very large volumes. To do this they must use the best persuasive skills available, via television, the press, radio and other advertising media. Gradually this influence has reduced, although we are all open to persuasion in what we buy.

After the Second World War, and because of the years of doing without, the consumer was hungry for products. The consumer was already tuned into persuasive advertising, due to the successful propaganda used during the war.

By the 1950s, the UK had begun to mirror the mass broadcasting that had already been so successful in the USA. By the late 1960s commercial radio was broadcasted throughout Europe.

As the new decade dawned, the UK entered a period of almost full employment and great prosperity. Commercial television was here, and with the rise in home ownership the UK consumer wanted every available domestic product.

From the 1970s, consumer legislation tackled all aspects of selling, from guarantees and advertising to credit. As the decade ended the consumer was demanding more and more from even the most basic products. The 1980s saw uncertainty about the future and the economy, and with it even greater demands for high quality and better specifications.

Today we see the chain stores dominating the market, and massive influence and power in the media, but a new force is in the arena. Consumer-led groups, set up to defend the rights of the public, flourish. There is a marked dislike of credit cards, poor-quality mass-produced goods and the dominance of large multi-nationals.

Green issues are very important. Not only do they address the excesses of industry and demand greater responsibility by manufacturers but they also urge the consumer to think more carefully about aspects such as recycling.

The consumer has, at times, been led by the manufacturer, but perhaps the balance has tilted in favour of the consumer. Consumerism demands change, not only for better service and quality, but for all aspects of products, distribution and selling. If an organisation does not fall foul of consumer legislation, it will surely attract the consumers' attention to its lack of response and ethical behaviour.

Pressure groups

Unlike political parties, pressure groups do not seek political power in the sense that they do not have parliamentary candidates. They are groups of like-minded people who try to influence the government. There are two main types of pressure group:

- *interest groups*, also known as *protective groups*. These groups protect the interests of a particular section of society (examples would include professional associations and trade unions)
- *cause groups*, also known as *issue groups*. These groups promote or support a particular cause (examples would include animal rights and environmental issues)

Pressure groups do provide the government with useful information that would not normally be available to them. They are extremely important for the following reasons:

- to help defend and support various minority interests
- to provide communication between the government and other decision makers between elections
- to help in the framing and implementation of government policy and legislation

During the health service reforms, the British Medical Association (BMA), who represent doctors and the various trade unions representing other workers in the health service, were closely involved in consultations aimed at improving the service to patients.

The government and these pressure groups work quite closely together at times. In certain areas this consultation can be quite formal, which would include:

- serving on advisory bodies
- membership of consultation groups
- membership of committees of enquiry
- membership of royal commissions

Much of the consultation is also undertaken informally. This includes:

- *off the record* meetings between government ministers and pressure groups
- the use of professional lobbyists
- *insider status* which means that the pressure group is regularly, though only informally, included in the decision making

The methods used by the various pressure groups to influence government decision making may differ, but typical actions could include some of the following:

- direct consultation
- negotiations or bargaining
- marches, strikes and demonstrations

Some of the larger and more established groups have a number of employees or experts who are able to advise and give an extra air of responsibility to these activities. Typical groups in this category would include:

- the Confederation of British Industry, who represent and support the employer's side of the argument

- the Trade Union Congress, who represent and support the employee's side of the argument

Untrue claims by business organisations

It is increasingly difficult for business organisations to claim things about their products and services that are either untrue or misleading. To this end, the first line of defence would be with the regulatory bodies which control the various forms of advertising and marketing. Assuming a bogus advertisement gets through this checking process, it will now face the full powers of the enforcement agencies.

Unsurprisingly, these products and services will, no doubt, be the subject of a large number of complaints. Arising from this, the local trading standards office will be extremely interested in the false claims made by the business organisation.

In the case of loss or injury as a result of the product or service not living up to the expectations of the consumer, there may be criminal proceedings against the organisation under the various pieces of legislation, including that on product liability.

Consumers are now much more aware of what it is reasonable to expect from a product or service. In this sense, outrageous claims about the product or service will be so obvious and outstanding that there will be little hope of the organisation actually getting away with it.

The media are also extremely interested in bogus claims. Newspapers, radio and TV have regular features which highlight the abuses and false descriptions of products and services.

▼

Focus study The Broadcasting Complaints Commission

This independent statutory body was set up in 1981. Its principal purpose is to consider and pass judgement upon complaints received about radio and television programmes. Its powers derive from the Broadcasting Act 1990.

The Commission considers complaints in the following categories:

- unjust or unfair treatment in radio and television programmes
- unwarranted invasions of privacy in such programmes

It considers complaints about all programming on the BBC (both TV and radio), the BBC World Service, ITV, Channel 4, Independent Radio and S4C. With the arrival of satellite and cable television, these too fall under the control of the Commission. It is also responsible for both advertisements and teletext services.

Complaints can be made by any individual or organisation. The unjust or unfair treatment refers to those who participated in the programme. Unwarranted invasion of privacy must be brought to the attention of the Commission by the person who has been infringed against.

Complaints are made in writing, either directly or after the complainant has unsuccessfully complained to the broadcasters.

The letter should go to the Secretary of the Commission, giving the title of the programme, the date and the channel on which it was broadcast.

The Commission will not consider a complaint if any of the following apply:

- the unjust or unfair treatment (or the infringement of privacy) is the subject of legal proceedings
- the complainant could take legal action
- the complaint is frivolous or inappropriate
- the broadcast was made some time ago
- the complainant does not have a sufficiently direct interest

If the Commission decides that the complaint should be investigated, then they send a copy of the complaint to the broadcaster. The broadcaster is then required to provide a transcript of the pro-

Fig. 5.3.1 The Independent Television Commission leaflet Advertising & Sponsorship on Commercial Television

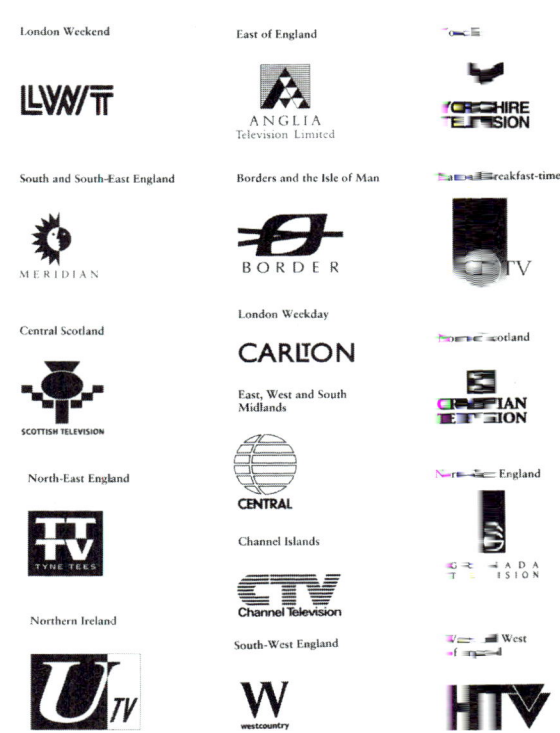

Fig. 5.3.2 The ITC regulates the services provided by all the regions

gramme along with a written statement answering the complaint.

The Commission may now have a private hearing and adjudicate. The procedure does take several weeks, and this is to give the broadcaster and the complainant the fullest opportunity to put their side of the case.

Dangerous products

When a product is patently dangerous to the consumer (i.e. the buyer or anyone who may use it), the organisation which supplied the product is leaving itself open to court proceedings. Even if we assume that the product was discovered to be dangerous *before* there was any damage done, the organisation is as much in the wrong and open to prosecution as it would have been otherwise.

There are countless sad cases of children and adults being killed or maimed by dangerous products every year. Even the most basic item may have killed or seriously injured someone in the past. Take a Bic disposal biro. Have you ever considered why it has a hole in the pen top? Some years ago a young child swallowed the pen top and could not breathe. Now, even if the pen top is swallowed, there is a ready-made air-hole for safety.

As we have said in the first element of this unit, providing the organisation is adhering to legislation or guidelines produced by the government or the EC, then no blame can be attached to them as far as product liability is concerned.

Such is the power of the consumer these days, that only the merest hint of a danger associated with a product will destroy or radically affect the sales and profitability of the supplier.

▼

Focus study
British Nuclear
Fuels

In a recent publication, British Nuclear Fuels (BNFL) stated its genuine desire to improve environmental performance through positive action.

The company, which employs over 15,000 people, supporting another 50,000 in British industry, has a £5.5 billion investment programme.

They manufacture and reprocess fuel for the UK's power stations which supply around a quarter of the country's electricity.

They state that they have been concerned with environmental care for many years. Their environmental policy covers:

- monitoring and managing the effluent discharges from their sites to ensure compliance with statutory limits and to help develop a strategy for further improvement
- the minimising of waste, together with recycling when possible
- efficiently using energy, raw materials and other resources
- monitoring the environment and assessing the effects of discharges
- managing their own land and property to improve the quality of the local environment
- publishing reports to ensure that the public are fully informed about the standard of their environmental performance

Unreliable services

Even with many organisations going out of their way to provide reliable and guaranteed services, it would be a mistake to think that in many cases the consumer does not end up with a bad deal.

Even with the best customer service, after-sales service, warranties and guarantees, the consumer is constantly faced with poor responses from businesses.

As we have detailed elsewhere, the services provided by a number of companies come *guaranteed* with a *customer service charter* or similar. In this respect, it is true that many organisations that were notorious for poor or slow service have vastly improved over the past few years.

This is by no means the whole story. Countless cases of unreliable services, not necessarily related to the product itself, occur on a weekly basis. The product may be good but the backup service and the promises of the supplier often fail to materialise.

Again, as we have mentioned earlier, there are some organisations who literally guarantee their services. Particular examples include:

- *Domino Pizzas*: who promise a free pizza if it is delivered later than promised (usually half an hour)
- *British Telecom*: who are rumoured to be paying out around £43,000 per day in compensation payments to their customers

5.3.2 EXPLAIN THE PURPOSES OF CONSUMERISM IN RELATION TO THE PROVISION OF PRODUCTS AND SERVICES

PURPOSES

Customers, obviously, demand that their requirements be met. They are always looking for benefits that a product or service can offer them. The key elements are always:

- having the right product available
- having the product available at the right price
- having the product available in as many places (outlets) as possible
- having the product in stock at all times, both in the warehouse and at the outlets

Customer expectations are a notoriously difficult thing to measure. It is only through continuous market research and the monitoring of customer's reactions to the products and services that an organisation can begin to build up a profile of the customer's expectations.

Some of the more obvious expectations can be addressed as a matter of course. Indeed, all organisations can identify the key expectations that relate to their particular area of business. Some of these expectations may include the following:

- accurate and reliable information about the product or service
- prompt and courteous advice and feedback regarding questions about the product or service

- the wide availability of the product or service
- consistency in the quality, style, colour or other standardised features of the product or service
- reliable and responsive after-sales service, maintenance or technical back-up after the purchase of the product or service
- good, competitive pricing structures that encourage the customer to return to the same organisation time and time again for the purchase of the product or service
- a consistent public image of the organisation that neither undermines nor embarrasses the customer

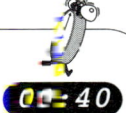

student activity

PC5.3.2 COM 2.1

In pairs, try to think of some other basic customer expectations. Are these expectations fair? Does the customer expect too much from the supplying organisation? How much real effort should be expended by an organisation in the pursuit of ensuring that customer's expectations are met and often exceeded? Once you have drawn up a list of expectations, discuss the other questions arising from this with the rest of the group.

Focus study
Insurance

Buying insurance can be very difficult. Getting it right can sometimes be impossible. The Office of Fair Trading offer some good advice:

- decide exactly what you want to have insured before contacting anyone
- once you have contacted a company find out exactly what their policy covers
- choose the one that suits you best
- watch out for exclusion clauses
- check whether you will have to pay the first part of the claim (this is called an excess)

Fig. 5.3.3 The Office of Fair Trading issues a useful leaflet which acts as a guide to household insurance

- when you have filled in an insurance form, make sure you keep a copy of it
- if you need to make a claim, then ask the building society, bank or insurance broker that you bought the policy from to help you

If you do have any complaints about your policy or the insurance company, then it would be wise to contact one of the following organisations:

- the Association of British Insurers: who deal with complaints about policies issued by member companies
- the Insurance Ombudsman Bureaux: who deal with disputes between member companies and their policy holders
- the Personal Insurance Arbitration Service: who may be used for independent arbitration using members from the Chartered Institute of Arbitrators
- the Lloyds Consumer Enquiries Advisory Department: who will deal with complaints relating to all aspects of policies issued by Lloyds Underwriters
- the Insurance Brokers Registration Council: who have issued a code of conduct to which all registered brokers must adhere

- the British Insurance Brokers Association: who are the trade body to whom brokers belong

Defence of consumer interests

Without doubt the consumer needs various consumer organisations to help notice, mobilise and act upon particular problems that could be against their interests.

Large businesses, government and various trade associations have an interest in trying to restrict choice, cut down on expenditure and generally improve their own position, to the loss of the consumer.

Consumerism has made us all much more aware of what is going on, what is available and, above all, what our rights are in certain circumstances.

With huge budgets, experts and a knowledge of the situation, the suppliers of products and services would be free to take advantage of the lack of power of each of us as individual consumers. With vigilant organisations who monitor and report back to the public, this is far less likely than in the past.

Like many things, the consumer interest against the wishes and needs of business is something of a balancing act. We cannot demand, as consumers, things that are impossible or would make the prospect of supplying these products and services to us unprofitable. On the other hand, profit has to be tempered with restraint and concern for the consumer, the environment and the law. The legislation that protects the consumer is one thing, but with the pace of technology, the law is often outstripped by the activities of the supplier. It is at this point that the consumer groups step in and provide the necessary protection – until the law catches up.

Focus study
The Food
Commission

A gradual and unpublicised change in the size of the tins of baked beans, soup and vegetables has cost consumers at least £10 million in hidden price rises. Trading standards officers, supported by a number of different consumer groups, have accused major food manufacturers of increasing prices by *down sizing* their tins.

Heinz, HP Foods and Crosse & Blackwell are all being accused of reducing the size of their tins without lowering the prices. The independent watchdog The Food Commission claim that millions of shoppers have been misled. The practice is alleged to have begun with Heinz, who cut the size of their tins of baked beans back in 1993 from 450g to 420g. Although this was a 7 per cent reduction in size, the 29p price tag remained the same. Bearing in mind that Heinz sell more than 500 million tins of baked beans every year (worth some 45 per cent of the £250 million market), they did not stop there. Soup was reduced from 435g to 405g, whilst tins of vegetables reduced from 220g to 205g.

It was not long before other food companies followed Heinz's lead. Crosse & Blackwell (owned by Nestlé) reduced the size of their baked beans from 440g to 420g, whilst tinned pasta shapes reduced from 425g to 410g. Again, there was no price reduction. Even own-label brands got in on the act. Their soups were reduced by 5 per cent from 420g to 400g. It was when the price came down by 8 per cent from 38p to 35p that the consumers began to realise what was going on.

The food industry responded by claiming that down sizing was simply a way of making some profit in an increasingly competitive market. Given the fact that some own-label brands have been sold for as little as 4p per can, there is little wonder why the companies attempted to mislead the customers. This, they emphatically deny. Their response to the accusations revolve around the standardisation of tins to fall in line with other European countries. Unfortunately for them, this

Fig. 5.3.4 *The Great Yarmouth and Waveney Health Authority produce their leaflet* A Simple Guide to Food Safety *for the use of their customers*

is not a legal requirement, and so despite their protestations, the down sizing was a very suspect manoeuvre.

Increase consumer influence

The organisation's long-term viability may very well depend upon the customers' perception of the organisation. In this respect we need to identify two key areas upon which the organisation needs to depend. These are:

- customer service
- marketing communications

Figure 5.3.5 attempts to act as a cross-referencing mechanism which measures the *relative organisational* versus *customer* orientation. *At location*

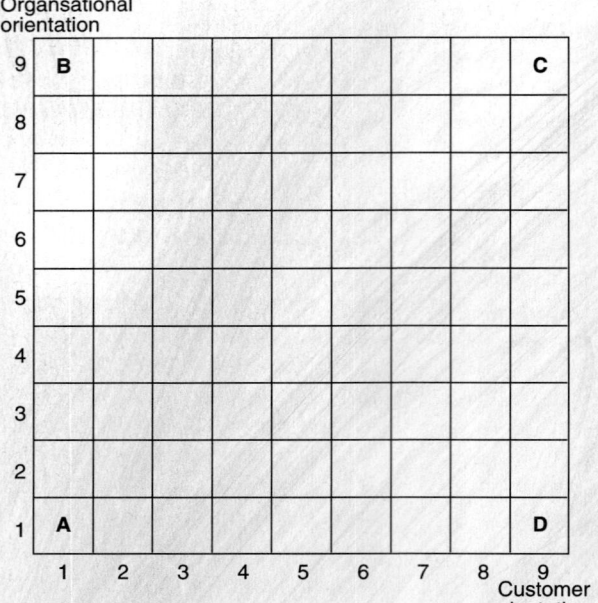

Fig. 5.3.5 Marketing Matrix

PC5.3.2
COM 2.1, 2.3
AON 2.1, 2.3

00:30

As a group, agree on 10 organisations with which you are all familiar. Having drawn up this list, then construct a marketing matrix and individually position the 10 organisations on the grid. Try to do this in secret, and once you have completed the task compare your results with those of the rest of the group.

A: the actions taken by the organisation are detrimental to both the organisation and its customers. Typically, the employees may be openly hostile to customers and have little motivation. This state of affairs may exist for organisations who do not have any direct competition. At *location B*: we have the ideal situation. The organisation has matched its objectives with the requirements of the customer. At *location C*: this is the ideal example of a product-orientated organisation. At *location D*: the organisation's employees are

rather too helpful and accommodating to customers.

The marketing communications methods operate as the first point of contact for the organisation with its potential customers. The nature, style, effectiveness and quality of the marketing communications methods employed will have a direct impact on the customers' perceptions of the organisation. Given the situation, when the marketing communications techniques used are deemed inappropriate or unappealing, the customers' perceptions of the organisation may well be undermined before the organisation has had a chance to convert any interest into sales. Conversely, if the organisation gets its marketing communications techniques right, then even the most sceptical or cynical customer may be encouraged to enter into a relationship with the organisation.

Improve products and improve services

The needs of the customer can be summarised by looking at the following considerations:

- the organisation must be able to establish what the customer's needs are
- the organisation needs to interpret them into clear needs
- the organisation needs to then mirror these needs in the production and distribution of products and services
- the organisation also needs to ensure that any products or services provided meet exacting quality standards in order to achieve long-term customer satisfaction and probable repeat sales

If there is one thing that will ensure that a potential customer becomes a non-customer, this is the non-availability of the product. If the customer either experiences difficulties in finding a stockist of a product, or, once having found this outlet, discovers that the purchasing process is complex, then they will turn to an alternative product and supplier. Obviously, to alleviate this potential problem and facilitate the immediate and simple purchasing process, the organisation must have chosen wisely in its distribution or sales channels. As we have discussed earlier, different products have different levels of availability, often related to some form of perceived exclusivity. This is also the case for products of a technical or complex nature, since only competent stockists with expert staff on hand can accurately match the product with the customer's needs.

The concept of the *one stop shop* has definitely arrived – particularly when we consider hypermarkets or supermarkets, which not only offer a wide range of consumable products but also offer dry cleaning, post office services, restaurants, petrol and even banking. The proximity of all these services is aimed at providing the customer with the easiest possible method of taking advantage of the variety available. Whilst this may have led to a downturn in the fortunes of city-centre and town-centre shopping, it has meant that there have been extensive developments in out-of-town or suburban sites. The alternative to the single shop system is the conglomeration of do-it-yourself, home furnishing, gardening, car parts and maintenance and electrical goods. With ease of parking and a short walk from store to store, this has proved to be an attractive alternative to the shopping mall or shopping centre. All these retail developments have been inherited from the *American experience*. Some have taken several years to *take off* and be embraced by the British public.

If we consider that the customer now has the choice of shopping locally, in a shopping centre, in an out-of-town site, by phone or from a catalogue, there appears to be no area that has not been exploited by manufacturers, suppliers and retailers. Shopping has never been easier or more simple. It is without doubt that shopping will become even easier in the future, particularly with the development of new telecommunications systems which enable the consumer to purchase a variety of goods from home.

There is a statutory or legal obligation for the organisation to provide clear and accurate information regarding their products or services. It is, however, advantageous for the organisation to make sure that the customer receives the highest level of information and accuracy before, during and after the sales process. Dependent upon the distribution or sales channel chosen by the organisation, this will be more or less in the control of the manufacturer or original supplier. Obviously, the more distance there is between the manufacturer or supplier and the end user, the less control the former has on the information transmission

system. In such situations, the manufacturer would be at pains to ensure that at every point or stage in the distribution process, sufficient information, in terms of either sales literature or training, is passed down from level to level. Some organisations either value the use of mass product briefing sessions to stockists or distributors of the product, or will support the sales force at the point of sale with regular visits by experienced sales representatives. The dissemination of printed material is essential and often undertaken with the assistance of the retail outlets. The joint publication of sales literature or mini-catalogues is fairly routine in this area.

If a customer is concerned with obtaining a refund or replacement, then the employee should be aware of the organisation's policy in these matters. If the employee does not have the authority to refund or replace, then they should always refer the matter to a senior member of staff who should be aware of the policy.

Some retail outlets will have special cash registers which are only used when money needs to be refunded to a customer. Marks and Spencer, who have a *no quibble* refund policy, are a particularly good example of this.

Research has shown that customers are more inclined to purchase from a retail outlet which provides a clear receipt, as this is not only proof of purchase but also a guarantee that a refund will be given if the product proves to be unsuitable in some way. It should be noted that refunds are generally given in the same manner as the payment was usually made, in other words, a cash sale is refunded in cash, but a credit card sale is refunded by the use of a credit card refund voucher.

As with refunds, there are occasions when a customer may request that a product be exchanged for another item of stock. Again, the employee will need to know the exchange policy of the organisation and should always check the item for signs of use, damage or missing parts. Providing the product appears to be in good order, then an exchange may be undertaken. This is, of course, assuming that the customer has some form of proof that they purchased the product from that retail outlet, or at least from part of the same chain of retail outlets. It is an all too common occurrence that certain individuals attempt to exchange goods purchased elsewhere, or perhaps obtained in a less legal manner, for other goods.

student activity `00:20`

In pairs, simulate your response to the following refund or replacement queries:

- a customer enters a record shop and produces a CD. The customer explains that this CD was purchased on their behalf by a friend as a birthday present. Unfortunately the customer already has this CD but has no means of proving that the CD was purchased in this shop.

- an elderly gentleman returns to a large do-it-yourself superstore. He is dragging behind him a petrol mower. Walking up to the customer service desk, he explains that the mower refuses to start. Upon questioning the procedures involved in starting the lawn mower, he confesses that he has filled the fuel tank with diesel.

- a customer returns to a car spares outlet, having purchased, only a matter of hours before, a can of undercoat spray. Having prepared the surface of his car and masked off the areas he did not wish to spray, he followed the instructions on the can and proceeded spraying onto the body work. He now has a red car with a large patch of bright green paint. The label had claimed to be white primer. Since the car is not very old, he is very annoyed.

- a young woman returns to a clothes shop clasping a carrier bag containing a dress. She has proof of purchase, and the garment was definitely purchased from this outlet. She purchased the garment very late on Saturday afternoon. It is now lunch time on Monday. She claims that she has changed her mind and does not like the garment any more. Upon close inspection the garment has a stain and shows signs of having been worn.

A customer may be dissatisfied for a number of reasons. These may include the following:

- the product which they purchased is faulty

- they require a product which either you do not stock or is out of stock
- they have received poor service
- they have a problem which nobody seems to be able to help them with

In many cases, organisations will have a formal complaints procedure for customers who are dissatisfied. It is usual practice for complaints to be referred to the manager, who is empowered by the organisation to act on behalf of them and make any on-the-spot decisions to help rectify the situation. There are some key stages here which, regardless of the formal complaints procedure, should be followed:

- when listening to the complaint, do not interrupt, and give the customer the opportunity to explain the situation
- always appear to be sympathetic to the customer
- in particularly complicated cases, make sure that you write down all the details
- when you have done this, check the main points of the complaint with the customer
- even if the customer is abusive, always try to remain calm and polite
- if you feel you cannot solve the situation yourself, keep calm and refer the matter to a senior member of staff
- never give the customer a vague response or an unbelievable excuse
- never blame anyone else directly
- even if provoked, do not lose your temper
- never try to infer that the complaint is not really a problem: in the eyes of the customer, it *is*
- always tell the customer exactly what you are going to do, particularly if this involves having to refer to another person or company
- above all, never make any promises which you cannot either personally fulfil or be sure will be fulfilled

When we consider that each customer is an individual in their own right, they may have a range of special needs which will require a different level of service. We can identify the following types of customer who may have special needs and attempt to look at any special services they may require. These are:

- *children* – unless you are involved in a retail

outlet, it is highly unlikely that day-to-day contact with children as customers will be normal. It is not always the case that these children will be accompanied by adults, and it is in this respect that children may require special levels of service. The child may not be able to communicate on an adult level and may need additional assistance when either choosing or paying for the product. However, it is always advisable to treat a child just as you would treat an adult, and you should not assume that because of their relatively tender age they are incapable.

- *special needs* – this rather broad category includes customers with hearing difficulties, the blind or partially sighted and the physically and mentally handicapped. Each will have their own particular requirements, and many retail outlets in particular have taken steps to ensure that both access and layout of the outlet facilitates ease of use.
- *foreign customers* – although the majority of overseas visitors may have some ability to speak and understand English, this may not be the case with overseas customers who are attempting to purchase products via the telephone. In larger organisations, attempts will have been made to identify employees who are able to speak foreign languages, and these individuals may be contacted in the event of any communication problems.

Quality standards

Quality Assurance (QA) is an attempt to ensure that the organisation adopts a series of quality standards that have been agreed as part of a system to achieve customer satisfaction. In essence, QA tries to address the following concerns:

- the time and effort put into product design
- the technology used in product design
- the quality of the components, materials and parts used
- the commitment and efforts of the employees
- the setting up of a system that monitors and records the quality issues associated with product design and production
- the assurance that the organisation can and will deliver on time with the correct orders of a suitably high level of quality
- the organisation is geared up to be able to offer

good advice before, during and after the sale has been made

An American writer L.P. Sullivan has identified seven stages to achieve organisation-wide quality control. He uses two shorthand terms throughout his appraisal of the quality-control process, and these are:

TQC – Total Quality Control: which means that there is a system in place that integrates all the different departments of an organisation in such a way as to ensure that the quality concept is standard and adopted by all parts of the organisation. The main aim, of course, is to achieve complete customer satisfaction with the product and all the allied and support systems offered by the organisation. The central issue for this concept is the management of quality-control systems which address the following:

- the specification of the product
- the customer's expectations of the product
- the balance between cost and quality

CWQC – Company-wide Quality Control: which aims to provide a good-quality, low-cost product to the customer. It goes further and states that the organisation should endeavour to offer benefits to the customers, employees and owners of the organisation by addressing their specific needs. CWQC refers to the following concerns:

- the quality of the management
- the quality of the human behaviour within the organisation in terms of how the individuals interact and co-operate with one another
- the quality of the working conditions and general environment
- the quality of the product itself
- the quality of the service

student activity `20:15`

PC5.3.2
COM 2.1

What do you see as the main differences between TQC and CWQC? Discuss this as a group.

The seven stages listed below are in relation to the two concepts outlined above. The first three stages relate to TQC and the fourth, fifth, sixth and seventh to CWQC. The seven stages are:

- *stage one* – the inspection of the product after production, with audits of the finished products. There will be problem-solving activities related to this which address the differences in quality at this stage and how to rectify them. This is known as being *product orientated*
- *stage two* – the quality assurance checking during the production process, which will include looking at the monitoring of statistical information that can help to identify slight variations in the quality of the product during the production process. This is a *process orientated* approach to quality assurance
- *stage three* – the checking of the systems used to monitor and maintain quality assurance in all departments within the organisation. This involves a *systems orientated* approach to the maintenance of quality assurance
- *stage four* – formulating and instituting a system which aims to make all the employees of the organisation think about the quality issues and be aware of the concept of quality assurance. This is known as a *humanistic approach*
- *stage five* – looking at the production and product design itself in order to discover a cheaper way of producing the product for the benefit of the organisation and the customers. This is called a *society orientated* approach
- *stage six* – this stage addresses the need to be cost conscious in the light of any fall in the quality of the product if the costs (or inputs) related to the product are reduced. This is called a *cost orientated* approach
- *stage seven* – this is the attempt to adapt the production process and the nature of the product itself to the needs of the customer and respond to their desires or instructions relating to that product. This is known as a *consumer orientated* approach

student activity `00:20`

PC5.3.2
COM 2.1

As a group, try to define exactly what would be done in each of the seven stages. Attempt to identify an example of the kind of actions that the organisation would take in relation to each of the different stages.

5.3.3 SUGGEST HOW CONSUMERISM BENEFITS BUSINESS ORGANISATIONS

BENEFITS TO BUSINESS

As a result of the introduction of the Consumer Protection Act 1987, businesses in the UK must make sure that they monitor and control the safety of the products they supply. This gives them additional incentive to make sure that the people using their products are able to rely on the safety aspects.

All organisations should, as a result of both the Consumer Protection Act and the rise of consumerism pressure in the UK, take the following steps which are beneficial to both the business and the consumer:

- review their management procedures to make sure that all checks are made during the design, manufacture, presentation and marketing of the products
- check that when existing standards are in existence they are applicable to their products
- introduce a quality assurance system such as BS5750
- assess whether their insurance cover is sufficient to cover, particularly, product liability insurance claims

Unsolicited feedback from consumers

Whether suppliers like it or not, they are subject to a steady stream of communication from their customers. Without prompting, or, indeed, without any clear name or address, consumers across the country routinely offer feedback on the quality and reliability of products and services.

Many organisations value this input and, to this end, have set up sections or departments which deal exclusively with the sifting and processing of mail received from their customers. On the positive side, these suggestions, which are often found within a letter of complaint, can offer valuable insights and ideas for the future. Other organisations, which choose to ignore this unsolicited feedback from customers, may find themselves consistently bombarded with the same type of complaint.

Although the vast majority of products and services have been extensively *road* or *crash* tested professionally, it is only when they are used on a long-term basis by a customer that unforeseen problems may arise. Although these problems may not be dangerous or significant in their own right, they do offer very useful suggestions which can be taken on board in the design of new products and services.

Basis for modification (of products, of services)

It is inevitable that by the time a product or service reaches the consumer, it is all but obsolete or out of date. Any organisation which adopts the policy of continuous product development will be at least one or two technological steps ahead of the product currently available in retail outlets. Whilst developing these products, a sensible organisation will attempt to eliminate the problems which have occurred in previous models. This forms a useful basis upon which to begin new product development. If previous problems can be avoided and new safety features incorporated, then the modification of products and services can be made all that much easier, largely due to the feedback received from consumers and consumer organisations.

Mutual understanding

As we will see in the last performance criteria of this element, business organisations will often employ public relations, community relations and other marketing methods in order to portray a caring and considerate image. Any organisation

would like to feel that they have got the consumer on their side. This can be achieved by gradual and careful development of their public image through a variety of different techniques. Amongst those which are more simple and straightforward to achieve are the publishing of leaflets and brochures together with relatively open access to visitors. Even in sensitive areas like nuclear fuel, British Nuclear Fuels (BNFL) are at great pains to appear approachable and environmentally friendly. Through various publicity stunts and long-term marketing campaigns, even the most hated and mistrusted organisation can attempt to portray the image of being misunderstood.

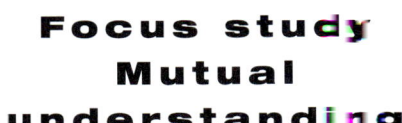

Focus study Mutual understanding

In a recent publication, Michael Jackaman, then the chairman of Allied Lyons plc, detailed his own version of mutual understanding. The highlights of his statement were:

'manufacturing industry makes a vital contribution to the wealth of the nation and has a responsibility to help build a healthy economic environment in which we may all enjoy an improving standard of living

The industry also has an obligation to carry out its activities in a way which neither squanders precious natural resources nor inflicts irredeemable damage upon the environment in which it operates. This balance of responsibilities is one which Allied Lyons has long acknowledged and one which we take very seriously.

We have millions of customers and to satisfy their needs calls for an ever increasing scale and variety of production processes – each with a potential cost in terms of waste and pollution.

Whether we are building a factory, redeveloping an existing site or installing new machinery, environmental concerns are fundamental and considered at the earliest stage of the planning process.

We are not, however, complacent. We realise that to play our part as good and responsible citizens calls for a commitment to the future as well as for the present.

We are committed to good environmental practice. Those efforts will continue and I hope you will be able to judge for yourself the extent of our success so far.'

▼

Focus study
The consumer and the utilities

Sharp rises in water bills and huge increases in profits, dividends and pay have provoked outrage. Only in telecommunications, where there is real competition, have customers seen big reductions. The domestic markets for gas, electricity and water are privatised monopolies where consumer pressure has come from the industry regulator.

Water bills have risen at double the rate of inflation since the industry was privatised in 1989, according to the Centre for the Study of Regulated Industries. The average domestic bill for un-metered water in England and Wales rose from £55.55 in 1989–90 to £88.03 in 1993–94, and the average sewage bill from £63.36 to £96.82. Official complaints have risen from 12.4 million in 1991–92 to just under 15 million in 1993–94. The water companies and OFTEL, the industry watch-dog, blame price rises on the need to fund heavy capital investment programmes to improve water quality.

British Gas claims that domestic prices fell by 20 per cent between December 1986 and July 1993, but VAT has reduced the cut to 14 per cent. Cedric Brown, chairman of British Gas, received a 75 per cent pay rise.

Electricity bills have risen from £237 in 1989–90 to £281 in 1994–95, although VAT on fuel has offset the benefits from lower prices. Annual complaints rose to 15,264, two years after privatisation, but have fallen since the companies agreed to pay out when service fell below certain levels. Directors have benefited from huge pay rises and share option schemes.

British Telecom's monopoly has been challenged by 150 competitors. BT claims domestic prices have fallen by 29 per cent as a result of price caps imposed by OFTEL, the industry regulator. The number of BT phone boxes has increased from 70,000 in 1984 to 128,000 and services have improved. Mercury, a main competitor, has announced plans to scrap its 9,600 phone boxes. BT's pre-tax profits rose from £1.5 billion in 1984 to £27.5 billion last year, and the workforce has been cut from 241,000 to 145,000. Directors' pay has rocketed.

BUSINESS ORGANISATIONS

Marketing plays an important role in enhancing the corporate or organisational image. An effective and well managed company should be market sensitive and aim to create greater customer satisfaction. Public relations cannot possibly succeed in its goals if the company is unable to show itself capable of performing well and demonstrating reasonable efficiency. Good trading performance, coupled with strong customer loyalty, goes a long way in maintaining a sound and positive corporate image.

Marketing can help the corporate or general image of the organisation in the following ways:

- *product publicity* – getting the products onto the TV or featured in newspapers and magazines
- *informing* – continually feeding information to the public and other interest groups
- *media relations* – co-ordinating advertising, sales promotions, press releases, etc. It is in the organisation's interest to release as much information as possible, to counteract any chance that the public misunderstands or has a negative impression of them
- *creating awareness* – fostering strong and positive attitudes to the organisation will help

add to the reputation of the organisation's products and services. If the brand name is well established and respected, then any problems associated with the organisation itself can be kept at a distance

- *developing the corporate image* – marketing can be involved throughout the whole process: from marketing research, that attempts to find out what the expectations towards the organisation are, to the analysis of customer behaviour. Targeting policies, advertising and selling and any attempt to readjust the perceptions of the organisation are also integral roles. But optimising the marketing opportunities and constantly pushing news of the organisation's successes should be tempered with the need to be honest if the organisation has made a mistake

The enhancement of product image encompasses many of the activities an organisation will employ to protect their market share or standing in the market. Promotions and sponsorships have become particularly popular in recent years. There are a number of organisations that have sponsored television programmes. The image of the television programme helps to enhance the customer's perceptions of the product.

National Power were unfortunate in their sponsorship of the 1990 World Cup. The unexpected defeat of the English team, which meant that they did not qualify for the finals, not only curtailed the television coverage but also damaged National Power's credibility. Martell Cognac, which sponsored the disastrous 1993 Grand National horse race, similarly suffered a loss of face as a result of the fiasco.

Private sector and public sector

Juggling the two considerations of *customer focus* and *organisational needs* may prove to be a constant problem for the organisation. In this section we will be considering the various ways of measuring the cost, effectiveness and impact of customer service against the sometimes conflicting requirements of the organisation itself.

There are, in effect, two very different approaches to business. One is known as the *market orientated* approach and the other is known as the *product orientated* approach.

A *market orientated* organisation has, in

essence, embraced the concepts of marketing. To these organisations, the customer is the most important aspect of the business. They will make strenuous efforts to make sure that the customer gets what they need. The entire organisation is geared up to provide for these needs, wants and aspirations of the customers.

A *product orientated* organisation, on the other hand, begins (not surprisingly) with the product. The form of the organisation's whole effort revolves around finding out the best ways to sell their products or services.

Let's restate these two opposing viewpoints and follow the logic behind each of the approaches. This is the approach of a *market orientated* organisation:

- What do people want?
- How many do they want?
- How much will they pay?
- Can we make a profit by providing for their wants?
- If we can, then we'll make them

The organisation is geared to the needs of the customer. It notes and acts on quality, reliability and price. In other words, the organisation is wholly *market orientated* and looks to that market to provide vital information about what it should produce.

The alternative view, and sadly a very common one, is the complete opposite. A *product orientated* organisation would change the sequence of questions to the following:

- These are the products that we can make, aren't they?
- Yes, we're good at that. Let's make more of them?
- Hang on, who are we going to sell them to?

- Never mind that, that's the sales peoples' job, isn't it?
- Great! That's true. Let's make some more, eh?

This approach does not take into account what the customer needs. The organisation only thinks in terms of what it makes and what it wants to do. If the organisation has produced something and they do not have a buyer, then the whole effort of the organisation switches to supporting the sales team. However, this might sound negative, but some organisations are really very good at operating in this way. They gear the whole organisation to selling and may even produce goods or services that the sales force feel *comfortable* selling.

▼

Focus study Customer orientation

The process of checking service excellence is becoming an increasingly important responsibility for management. British Airways, whose reputation and profitability was at rock bottom in the early 1980s, initiated their *putting people first* campaign into action and has reaped considerable benefits.

IBM, for example, has suffered from telling its customers what they need rather than asking them what they want. Their pre-eminence in the market has probably suffered irreparable damage. Del Computer Corporation, a $2 billion American computer manufacturer, has seen sales grow at up to 100% per year. By offering the twin benefits of *direct-from-manufacturer sales* and *unlimited telephone problem-solving support*, they have become extremely customer orientated. They have identified 16 major requests that customers make of them and have taken steps to make their response as efficient as possible.

When we consider the organisation's need to achieve and sustain productivity in relation to the level of customer service it offers, we are, perhaps, focusing on time. If we assume that the organisation is committed to customer service, then we must also assume that they are prepared to invest employees' time in seeking this satisfaction. It should be remembered that whilst an employee, particularly in the case of a retail assistant, is dealing with a customer-service-related issue, then they are not available to close other sales of a more straightforward nature with other customers. Equally, a salesperson who is dealing with a complex customer-service enquiry, is unavailable to take calls or enquiries that may result in a more profitable sale. To this end, it has become apparent to many organisations that there is a need for a discrete customer service section. These individuals will field the bulk of complex enquiries or complaints, only referring them to the *front line staff* when they cannot handle the situation themselves.

We should also consider the case of individuals working in a manufacturing environment, who may be constantly interrupted by visitors who require customer service on an immediate basis. Again, whilst handling these enquiries, the employee cannot proceed with their own tasks and duties. In all these cases, assuming that the organisation does not have a discreet customer service section, productivity will be lost.

There needs to be some kind of balance established between the need to provide *customer service* and the *productivity requirements* of the organisation. The other aspect which is involved here is that in smaller firms, where individuals undertake a wide range of different duties, they cannot be expected to perform routine tasks if they are constantly bombarded with customer-service problems.

Turning to *profitability* in relation to customer service, it has been established that if the organisation manages to retain the customer for a considerable period of time, then that customer's business with the organisation becomes increasingly more profitable. Loyal customers who make repeat sales offer the following benefits:

- their spending will increase over a period of time
- they may purchase other products offered by the organisation
- they are likely to recommend or refer friends or acquaintances to the organisation
- they are less price-sensitive than new customers

Against this is the fact that loyal customers may

cost more to acquire in the early stages of the organisation's relationship with them. This is more than outweighed by the additional benefits mentioned above, as well as the probable savings in terms of reduced day-to-day customer-service costs relating to that customer and the inevitable costs incurred if that customer should be lost.

On the subject of *accountability*, we return to the thorny problem of actually assessing the potential income derived from customer-service activities. It is very difficult to identify whether sales achieved from existing customers were as the result of their normal spending intentions or whether they were as a result of customer service. Obviously it very much depends on who you are or where you are in the organisation. Those involved in customer service would claim that these increased sales were as a result of their own efforts, whilst the sales department would claim that *they* can take credit for the sales.

▼

Focus study
Cost of customer service versus accountability

As we have mentioned in this section on accountability and customer service, it is often difficult to try to set some kind of value to the process of customer service. However, Coopers and Lybrand, a management consultancy firm, have suggested that around 60 per cent of all complaints by a business customer have nothing to do with the product itself. The way in which customers are handled is the most common cause of customer complaints.

Rather than being irritated by complaints, organisations need to learn that complaints can give them important feedback. Research has shown that out of any 100 complaints from dissatisfied customers, only four are seasoned complainers who will complain about anything regardless of the level of service. Of the 100 complaints, 25 will defect to the competition and 75 per cent of these will never return. Perhaps the worst aspect is that

the 10 lost customers will tell up to 20 other people each about their dissatisfaction.

Large, medium and small business organisations

There has always been a certain degree of scepticism surrounding the measurability of public-relations activities. The common way of measuring the effectiveness of public relations exercises was to look at the number and length of articles and news stories written about the organisation. How many times the organisation's name or products were mentioned in the media served as the only method of measurement.

It is true to say that public relations is one of the more intangible aspects of marketing, but after all, what is the difference in trying to measure the effectiveness of advertising over the effectiveness of public relations? The biggest difference, without doubt, is the amount of money organisations are prepared to spend on either activity. Public relations is the poor relative in this respect.

▼

Focus study
Public relations

Tracking the effectiveness of a public-relations (PR) exercise can be somewhat easier if you investigate a single issue event. National *No Smoking Day* relies entirely on public relations and has consistently achieved success it has achieved awareness levels of around 80 per cent of the adult population without any advertising back-up. The real value of the public-relations exercise has to be measured in terms of how many people give up smoking as a direct result of the public-relations campaign. In 1993, some two million people took part in *No Smoking Day* and around 50,000 are still not smoking.

The main targets of the public-relations effort are:

Performance Indicators 1994-95

All local authorities in England and Wales have to publish details, through a newspaper, of their performance in providing services. The indicators for assessing performance are laid down by the Audit Commission.

Under the Citizen's Charter everyone has the right to know how their Council is peforming and whether it is giving value for money.

The Citizen's Charter is a commitment to raising the standard of public services and making sure that services really do meet the needs and wishes of the people who use them.

Hamish McFarlane, Chief Executive,
Mid Suffolk District Council,
High Street, Needham Market, Suffolk IP6 8DL.
Telephone Needham Market: (01449) 720711
Fax: (01449) 721946 Minicom: (01449) 727120

MID SUFFOLK
District Council

Fig. 5.3.6 All local authorities have to publish details of their performance on an annual basis. The figure shows the performance indicators of the Mid-Suffolk District Council for 1994–95

HOUSING

PROVIDING FOR THE HOMELESS

PAYMENT OF BENEFITS

Points to note:

• **Repairs** - not all housing repairs are prioritized because some of the work, particularly routine work, can be carried out as part of long-term programmed maintenance.

• **Appointments** - whenever a tenant asks for a housing repair, we consider this as a request for an appointment and we visit the property. If access cannot be gained on the first visit, our contractor must leave a call card inviting the tenant to indicate a time when access can be gained.

• **Homelessness** - not all homeless persons are entitled to re-housing by the Council. We assist wherever we can but we must be satisfied that the homelessness is not wilful.

THE COUNCIL'S HOUSING STOCK	94/95	93/94
Number of dwellings managed by the Council at 31 March 1995	4,241	4,337
Percentage of these dwellings adapted for elderly or disabled people	41.2%	40.2%
Number of flats in blocks of 3 storeys or over, managed by the Council at 31 March 1995	42	Not available
Percentage of these flats with controlled entry	86%	Not available
Allocations and Lettings	**94/95**	**93/94**
Number of the Council's own dwellings let to new tenants	188	191
Number of successful nominations made to housing associations	51	39
Percentage of lettings and nominations that went to homeless households	39%	48%
Percentage of new lettings that went to other categories	61%	52%
Percentage of dwellings empty and available for letting or awaiting minor repairs at 31 March 1995	0.16%	0.27%
Average time taken to re-let dwellings available for letting or awaiting minor repairs (in calendar days)	24 days	22 days
Percentage of the housing stock empty because of major repairs	0.12%	0.42%

REPAIRS TO COUNCIL'S HOUSING STOCK	94/95	93/94
Total number of requests for repairs	16,726	22,314
Number of repairs requested under each priority level set by the Council:		
Emergency	1,065	1,035
Urgent	5,732	8,530
Routine	6,318	12,749
The Council's target response times under each priority level:		
Emergency	immediate	
Urgent	within 48 hours	
Routine	within 6 weeks	
Percentage of jobs completed within target times:		
Emergency	100%	100%
Urgent	62%	82%
Routine	87%	97%
Appointments for repairs	**94/95**	**93/94**
Percentage of repair jobs for which an appointment was offered	100%	100%
Percentage of repair jobs where an appointment was made because access not gained on first visit	2%	3%
Percentage of follow-up appointments kept by the Council	90%	95%

PROVIDING FOR THE HOMELESS	94/95	93/94
Number of homeless households placed in temporary accommodation on 31 March 1995	6	9
Type of accommodation given: Bed and Breakfast accommodation	1	4
Hostel accommodation	4	3
Other temporary accommodation	1	2
Average length of stay in temporary accommodation	38.5 days	81 days
THE COST OF MID SUFFOLK'S HOUSING	**94/95**	**93/94**
Average level of capital expenditure per dwelling on major repairs and improvements	£349	£672
Average weekly rent per dwelling at 31 March 1995	£37.93	£34.59
Average weekly cost per dwelling, itemised as follows:	**94/95**	**93/94**
Management	£6.97	£6.71
Repairs	£9.96	£8.25
Bad debts	£0.13	£0.02
Empty properties	£0.22	£0.15
Rent rebates	£20.40	£18.57
Financing of Capital Expenditure	£12.64	£12.64
Other items (net)	(£0.82)	£0.52
Total costs	**£49.50**	**£46.55**
Less Government Subsidy	(£11.57)	(£12.26)
=Average Weekly Rent	**£37.93**	**£34.59**

RENT COLLECTION	94/95	93/94
Percentage of rent collected compared to total amount due	98.8%	99.4%
Percentage of tenants owing over 13 weeks rent at 31 March 1995, excluding those owing less than £250	1.49%	0.85%

PAYMENT OF HOUSING BENEFIT AND COUNCIL TAX BENEFIT	94/95	93/94
Number of new claims for Council Tax benefit	2724	1563
Percentage of new claims processed within 14 days	88.0%	99.5%
Number of new claims for Housing Benefit from Council tenants	895	759
Percentage of new claims from Council tenants processed within 14 days	89.1%	84.3%
Number of successful new claims for Rent Allowance	1065	439
Percentage of new claims for Rent Allowance paid within 14 days	97.1%	91.3%
Total number of claimants for Benefit	5813	5573
Gross cost of administration per benefit claimant	£57.63	£64.9

To keep down the cost of publishing our Citizen's Charter performance indicators, we have condensed the necessary information into this four page leaflet, including a comparison with our performance for 1993/94. However, if you find the size of print difficult to read then please telephone: (01449) 727371 and we will send you a booklet (free of charge) containing a fuller version of the information in larger print.

Fig. 5.3.6 (continued)

- *the general public*: often targeted by community-relations exercises such as sponsorship events
- *the company's employees*: increasingly important, as the workforce is perceived as an asset rather than a necessary evil or potential source of confrontation
- *the banks and the stock exchange*: to whom the organisation must look to be financially sound and have good prospects
- *the customers of the organisation*: for whom PR must run alongside the advertising and general marketing policy. The education of customers as to the superiority of a product or service is vital, as well as maintaining general interest and awareness in the target group
- *the media*: an integral part of a well-organised PR campaign, as the organisation is keen to strike up a good relationship with the press, television or radio

Some typical forms of PR are detailed later, but let us look at the more general tasks that PR aims to perform:

identifying specific interest groups: which will be able to influence the public towards the organisation. The organisation will have to identify the objectives of these interest groups and assess the resources that are available to them. Examples of interest groups are *pressure groups* and *investors*. Once the interest group has been identified, the group's attitude to the organisation must be ascertained. How does the interest group operate? What are its strengths? The PR operation must form part of a plan to influence the interest group and project a favourable image to them. The organisation must also be able to deflect any criticism levelled at it by the interest group

counselling and advice: should be offered to the management of the organisation. The organisation should also be kept updated on their attitudes and opinions, as perceived by the general public and interest groups. The creation of forecasts of what might happen in the future should be a vital part of this in order to enable the organisation to respond positively and offset potential problems and criticisms

publicising the organisation's products and activities: this is an integral part of the overall marketing policy and duties. PR plays an important role in the launch of a new product and can be a key factor in the development of new ideas. PR aims to keep interested parties informed of trends, developments and launches on a continual and rolling basis

in the area of media relations: the PR element of the organisation needs to try to get press, radio or TV coverage. The media can be used to educate or inform the public about a certain product, service or activity with which the organisation is involved. Good examples of these are the use of Richard Branson's media-grabbing skills by Virgin and Anita Roddick's adeptness in pushing the Body Shop message home to the general public. As we will see shortly, the use of press releases is ideal in this respect

creating awareness and a positive attitude: doing so towards the organisation on a corporate level is extremely useful. This activity seeks to increase the overall interest and awareness that is not specifically related to a particular product or service. The use of sponsorship, as we will see, can help this cause immensely

lobbying the decision-makers: in both government and professional organisations, to persuade them to promote legislation, regulations, codes of practice or attitudes that are favourable to the organisation

A *press release* is a public-relations statement issued to the media by the organisation. The intention is to gain some editorial coverage that is favourable to the organisation.

When the organisation has a news item, the organisation will either write the press release themselves or engage the services of a professional marketing agency to write it on their behalf. The main aspects of writing a successful press release are:

- the press release sticks to the facts
- the press release is brief
- the contents of the press release are summarised in the first paragraph
- the press release contains the organisation's

ITC: Watching over commercial television

Fig. 5.3.7 This extract from the ITC leaflet
Watching Over Commercial Television
shows that advertising and
sponsorship is regulated

Watching over commercial television

Regulating programmes

We monitor programme content against a published set of guidelines, which apply to all commercial channels and are available to anyone. The main areas they cover are:

- taste and decency;
- the 'family viewing policy' - programmes shown before the 9pm 'watershed' on ITV and Channel 4 should be suitable for family audiences. The later they come after the watershed, the more adult they're allowed to be. Broadly the same policy applies to cable and satellite programmes, but there are different watersheds for certain subscription channels;
- behaviour children might imitate - for instance, we don't allow scenes

showing the dangerous use of knives before the watershed;

- impartiality and political balance - for instance, television news and current affairs are not allowed to express editorial opinions in the way newspapers do;
- giving undue screen time to branded products or services in programmes;
- the way programmes are made - for instance, there are rules on when it is and isn't acceptable to film members of the public without their knowledge;
- responsible treatment of issues and beliefs in religious programmes.

Regulating advertising and sponsorship

Like programmes, television commercials have to meet our published guidelines.

- They have to be legal, decent, honest and truthful.
- The amount of advertising and frequency of commercial breaks is restricted.

- Some products and services are forbidden from advertising - guns and cigarettes, for instance.
- Sponsors of programmes must be suitable for the programme concerned, and there are detailed rules about how and when their credits can be shown.

What if companies don't meet these standards?

In the case of programmes, we can require the television company to broadcast an apology. In more extreme cases we can issue a formal warning; worse offences may lead to a fine, and if a company persistently fails to meet our standards we can

shorten or even take away its licence.

In the case of advertisements, we can also ask for changes - or we can ban the offending advertisement outright.

We make a point of publishing our findings.

How do we set standards?

Our guidelines can't be set in tablets of stone; they have to reflect public tastes and attitudes, which are constantly evolving. So we keep them up-to-date in several ways. We conduct year-round audience research into

people's views and attitudes. We're advised by panels of viewers around the country. And we have expert advisory committees in specialist areas such as advertising, education, religion and medical issues.

What to do if you have a complaint or suggestion...

We don't just wait to hear views from the public; we monitor programmes and advertisements to see if they meet our standards. But we do take note of every comment we get from viewers, so if you make a

complaint or suggestion, we'll consider it - and let you know the outcome.

Before you contact us, though, make sure it's about something within our powers. Check the list overleaf of things we don't do...

name and telephone number, and gives a contact name

- the press release contains a quotation from the person responsible for the item. This gives a human angle to the press release.
- a photograph should be attached, if relevant, to increase the chances of the press release being used

It is also a good idea to try to get to know the editor or some of the journalists at the newspaper or magazine that would possibly feature your organisation. If the organisation has a news story, then an initial phone call should be made to offer an *exclusive* to the newspaper. This might be preferable to sending out a number of press releases to several different newspapers.

An organisation should also try to send articles and press releases to the trade press in the hope that they might feature the organisation's news or developments.

It is always worth trying to remember that the better the press release, the better the chances of the newspaper using it. Also, if the press release is written like a news story, then there is every chance that the story will be printed in full. Journalists are busy people, and if you make their jobs easier for them, then you have a great advantage.

In the UK, businesses spend around £250 million sponsoring sport each year. This figure is growing by about 10 per cent per year. According to the organisation Sports Marketing Strategy, sponsorship accounts for some 5 per cent of all of the advertising spending worldwide. Although sports advertising is aimed at reaching a mass audience, it is argued that since so many sponsorship deals are being struck, this dilutes the effect. When was the last time you bought something after seeing the name of a business or a product on the chest of your favourite sports personality?

Sports sponsorship is more than just image building. It is about selling products too, but the former is the more dominant. When a client has been sold on the concept of sponsorship, there are media-monitoring exercises carried out to indicate the exposure levels which measure the success or failure of the venture. Sponsorship supporters do admit that not enough research is being carried out to measure the real objectives of the sponsorship or, for that matter, the possible up-turn in sales as a result.

Normally, the business, product or brand is tracked against the trends in the market to try to show what effect the sponsorship had. Sponsorship is very strong on brand-building. Once the target market has been identified, the business will know a lot about the target group, their lifestyles, income and age, etc. If the target group is young and active, then the business would be wise to associate themselves with an active and exciting sport.

For some businesses, sponsorship deals that run to £750,000 or so are really just *petty cash* when you consider the massive advertising spending that may be going on at the same time. TV sponsorship has really come of age in the last few years. Just over half of advertisers and agencies are more likely to consider the possibilities of sponsoring TV programmes than a year ago. They now view the value of sponsorship as being extremely useful for brand enhancement and targeting specific markets and audiences.

Although around 80 per cent of advertisers state that they do not have a specific sponsorship budget, they also state that if they do use sponsorship then the costs are not taken out of the advertising budget. The main reasons for advertisers not to consider sponsorship are:

- poor targeting possibilities (i.e. of the audience type)
- budgetary restrictions of the business
- over-pricing of the sponsorship deal
- lack of control over how their name/brand will be used

Some 42 per cent of advertisers claim that TV sponsorship helped to build brand awareness, and 56 per cent said that it improved the image of the business. Some of the more prominent TV sponsorship deals in 1994 were:

Passengers (C4)	Pepsi
Don't Forget Your Toothbrush (C4)	Polaroid
Italian Football (C4)	Carlsberg Export
NFL (C4)	Budweiser
The Word (C4)	Swatch
Gamesmaster (C4)	McDonald's
World Cup (ITV)	Panasonic

Play Your Cards Right (ITV)

The Sun

You Bet (ITV)

Daily Mirror

Focus study
Sponsorship

Sponsors paid more than £152 million to be associated with the World Cup Finals in 1994. That figure appears to be very small when we consider the amount that the top 19 World Cup sponsors invested in advertising over the same period. This support advertising ran to a staggering £6.6 billion worldwide!

The returns were great too: some 31 billion people watched the World Cup Finals worldwide. However, the fact that England failed to make the finals cost an estimated £30 million in lost advertising. The USA was the big market that the sponsors wished to have an impact upon. The organisers of the World Cup, aware that football was a rather unknown and unloved sport compared to baseball, American football, ice hockey and basketball, spent an estimated £20 million on promoting the event to the Americans.

The two-tier sponsorship deals managed to attract some of the household names such as Coca-Cola, McDonald's and General Motors (each paying between £10 million and £13 million). The second tier, or *marketing partners*, paid around £4.6 million each.

McDonald's final bill, in sponsorship-related costs, ran to £46 million. They were more than pleased with their investment, for they believed that it would have been impossible to have gained the exposure that the World Cup gave them without that level of spending.

The term *lobbying* takes its name from a political activity which involves trying to influence members of parliament in the lobby (entrance hall) of the Houses of Parliament. In business terms, lobbying takes on a more wide role and involves the practice of attempting to influence any decision-maker for the benefit of the organisation or the industry in general.

It is at this, the industry or trade level, that the majority of lobbying is undertaken. Federations or associations that represent a particular trade or industry will act on their members' behalf to try to obtain a higher profile and become part of the decision-making process. They will attempt to become advisers to government or other bodies, being consulted when there is an issue that affects the industry.

Large organisations may well have a dedicated community-relations department. The main feature of this form of marketing is to heighten the awareness of the organisation within the local community, as well as to support local charities and issues.

This relatively cheap form of marketing or public relations can bring very positive benefits to the organisation in helping to mobilise support for the organisation. The feeling that the organisation is an integral part of the local community needs to extend beyond the obvious job-providing role. Many smaller communities may be economically reliant upon one or two businesses, and the organisation needs to be seen as a positive aspect of the local community and not just a job provider.

Charitable donations and other community-relations exercises are very good for the organisation's general image. If the organisation chooses the right kind of cause or event, then they can expect great dividends from this relatively cheap method of marketing.

Visits and open days are very useful methods too: by inviting the public to view the organisation, they can help improve the public's understanding of what the organisation is about. The Body Shop, for example, encourages the public to have a look at their operations, and they have regular guided tours of their premises in Littlehampton. To interest the visitors, there are exhibits, original packaging and a mock-up of the first Body Shop. The tour begins and ends at the Body Shop retail outlet on the factory site, where the public can buy products and merchandise that are not available anywhere else.

▼

Focus study Community relations (charity fund-raising)

The Flora Aerobathon 94, held in April, was a disastrous flop. In 1993, some 26,000 people were attracted to the London venue alone without the benefit of a significant advertising spend. In 1994, despite a £1.2 million advertising budget, only 17,000 people turned up to the five venues.

Flora had expected around 140,000 people, and had projected that the event would raise some £3 million for six national charities.

Publicity was carried on 55 million flora margarine tubs, with TV advertising in most areas and additional radio advertising in others. The event turned out to be the biggest flop in living memory. The Aerobathon collapsed with debts of over £1.2 million. The income raised from the nation-wide event amounted to only £340,000.

The charities had agreed to *write off* the first £150,000 per venue to cover the costs of the event. Initially, there was to have been six venues, so the total write-off would have been £900,000. This would have contributed greatly to the estimated £1.5 million costs of the whole event. The Royal Marsden Hospital was to receive the first £500,000. This meant that the event would have had to total some £1.25 million before any of the other charities got a penny.

Flora itself is one of the creditors, being owed some £300,000. At least they received the publicity and the increase in brand awareness. Other creditors were not so lucky: they face financial disaster.

assignment

In this final assignment of the Unit, you will have to follow through the information that we have already outlined and examine the effects of consumers on the provision of goods and services.

TASK 1 PC 5.3.1

Explain the reasons for the growth in consumerism.

TASK 2 PC 5.3.2

Explain the purposes of consumerism in relation to the provision of goods and services.

TASK 3 PC 5.3.3

Suggest how consumerism can benefit three different organisations.

NOTES

You will find valuable information about consumerism from newspaper articles, texts, journals and magazines. You should detail at least one local organisation and see how that has been affected by consumerism. You may find that this element assignment fits in very well with the one that you need to do for Unit 3, Element 3 of the mandatory part of this programme.

Index